Helping Others

Helping Others

Anthony R. D'Augelli
Pennsylvania State University

Judith Frankel D'Augelli

Steven J. Danish
Pennsylvania State University

Brooks/Cole Publishing Company
Monterey, California

Brooks/Cole Publishing Company
A Division of Wadsworth, Inc.

© 1981 by Wadsworth, Inc., Belmont, California 94002. All rights reserved. No part of this book may be reproduced, stored in a retrieval system, or transcribed, in any form or by any means—electronic, mechanical, photocopying, recording, or otherwise—without the prior written permission of the publisher, Brooks/Cole Publishing Company, Monterey, California 93940, a division of Wadsworth, Inc.

Printed in the United States of America

10 9 8 7 6 5 4 3 2

Library of Congress Cataloging in Publication Data

D'Augelli, Anthony R
 Helping Others.

 Bibliography: p.
 Includes index.
 1. Helping behavior. I. D'Augelli, Judith Frankel, joint author. II. Danish, Steven J., joint author.
 III. Title.
 BF637.H4D28 158'.3 80-17819
 ISBN 0-8185-0401-3

Acquisition Editor: *Claire Verduin*
Project Development Editor: *Ray Kingman*
Manuscript Editor: *Julie Segedy*
Production Editor: *Patricia E. Cain*
Interior Design: *Jamie Sue Brooks*
Illustrations: *Carl Brown*
Typesetting: *Linda Andrews, Ashland, Oregon*

Preface

For many years, the words and actions of helpers were cloaked in professional secrecy, and prospective helpers and helpees alike had little concrete sense of the process of helping others. During their graduate training, for example, the authors were exposed to *theories* of helping but learned what to say to helpees only by often painful trial and error. Recently, the helping professions have taken broad steps away from the mystery of helping and the "sink-or-swim" methods for training helpers. Our goal in this book is to aid in demystifying the helping process by presenting a comprehensive, skills-oriented approach to helping.

Helping Others is concerned both with the words and actions of helpers and with their effects on the helping relationship. We explore the importance of the helper's needs, values, and beliefs. Nonverbal messages conveyed by the helper's behavior are explored. Verbal behaviors that convey understanding, support, influence, questioning, and direction are reviewed. We discuss the ethics of helping others and how to integrate one's behaviors, beliefs, and personality into an effective and comfortable helping style. Since we believe that it is important to learn what to say in helping, we have provided sample dialogues. We have also included thought questions at the end of each chapter; these should provoke further discussion of the complexities of helping. This book should be useful to anyone beginning a helping career—in such areas as clinical psychology, counseling, social work, nursing, rehabilitation, and other human services—and to anyone wishing a basic orientation to helping others.

On the other hand, one cannot learn to be a helper from a book alone. Rather, intensive training in helping skills is needed. Our model of helping was derived from a training program described in *Helping Skills: A Basic Training Program* by Steven J. Danish, Anthony R.

D'Augelli, and Allen L. Hauer (New York: Human Sciences Press, 1980). To complement *Helping Skills,* this book provides an analysis of the rationale for the use of various helping skills, a description of additional helping strategies, and a discussion of the ethics of helping. Readers who are planning to enter a helping field would benefit from going beyond a reading of this book to the training provided by the *Helping Skills* program.

We would like to start this book with a note of modesty. We do not pretend to have the only model of helping, nor do we feel that our model is a new discovery. We have a model that is useful in teaching skills to future helpers because it breaks down complex concepts into discrete helping behaviors. It avoids some of the needless complexities of past efforts but still relies on the contributions of many in the helping fields to complement our own work. We have used this model to help people, and we hope that others will work with this perspective to make it even more useful.

Throughout the book, we use the word *helpee* to refer to all those people—clients, patients, friends, relatives, acquaintances, and strangers—who can be aided by a helper in formal or informal contacts. The choice of this word reflects the generic nature of the model of helping we describe.

One of the few pure joys of completing a book is the thanking of the many people who helped throughout the process of transforming ideas into print. Listing all those who contributed to our thinking would be impossible. How do you thank the hundreds of students whose challenges clarified your thinking? How do you thank a colleague whose cranky criticism pointed out illogic? Suffice it to say that this book reflects many years of spirited exchange with students and faculty in the Division of Individual and Family Studies at Penn State. The Division's commitment to the training of helpers provided the reasons for this book and the testing ground for the book's ideas.

Some specific people were immeasurably helpful in completing *Helping Others.* Without the highly professional help of Diane Bernd, Joy Barger, and Sarah Barber, *Helping Others* would remain a hopeless heap of handwritten thoughts. Without the constant support of Claire Verduin of Brooks/Cole, we would have abandoned the task of shaping our ideas into prose. We also appreciate the help of Ray Kingman of Brooks/Cole in bringing this project to completion. There is no doubt that these people were unusually helpful in making a sometimes frustrating process bearable. Also extremely helpful were the reviewers of earlier versions of the manuscript: Marlene S. Chrissinger, University of Nevada, Las Vegas; James G. Dugger, John A. Logan College, Carterville, Illinois; David D. Foat, University of Minnesota, Minneapolis; Allen E. Ivey, University of Massachusetts, Amherst; Bernice Podel, California State University, Chico; Ronald Schmidt, Los Rios Community College District, Sacramento, California; Paul F. Stegner, Canada College, Redwood City, California; George W. Watson, California State University, Fullerton; Sheldon D. Weinstock, Community College of Baltimore, Maryland; and Catharine S. Zimmerman, Camden County College, Blackwood, New Jersey. We finally wish to thank Rebecca L. D'Augelli for patiently delaying her birth until the final draft of *Helping Others* was ready to be sent to the editors. Her sister, Jennifer H. D'Augelli, meanwhile provided many opportunities to practice helping in myriad ways. Pamelyn Hoy and Kimberly Staub likewise provided much appreciated helping skills to all the D'Augellis throughout the writing and production of the book.

Anthony R. D'Augelli
Judith Frankel D'Augelli
Steven J. Danish

Contents

Chapter 1
A Conception of Helping   1

A Historical Sweep   1
Helping—A Definition   5
Promoting Change through Helping: An Equation   8
The Helping Process   11
Summary: "What Is Help?" Revisited   13
A Final Note   13
Thought Questions   14

Chapter 2
Helpers Are People Too   15

Needs   16
Beliefs and Values   26
Summary   27
Thought Questions   28

Chapter 3
You Are What You Do:
Nonverbal Behavior in Helping   29

What Should Be Communicated Nonverbally?   30
How Do Verbal and Nonverbal Behaviors Relate?   35
What Is Effective Nonverbal Behavior?   37

Situational Cues   39
Interactive Cues   42
Environmental Cues   50
Summary   52
Thought Questions   53

Chapter 4
The Words of Helping:
I. Continuing and Leading Responses   55

The Core Conditions: Definitions and Functions   57
Continuing Responses   62
Leading Responses   72
Summary   83
Thought Questions   84

Chapter 5
The Words of Helping:
II. Self-Referent Responses   85

Two Definitions   86
Why Talk about Oneself?   87
Authenticity or Selfishness?   93
Self-Involving   100
Summary   102
Thought Questions   102

Chapter 6
Understanding Others' Communications   103

The Process of Understanding   105
Global Understanding   107
An Example   110
Deep Understanding   112
Summary   123
Thought Questions   123

Chapter 7
Helping Strategies   125

Assessment   128
Planning   134

General Behavior Change Methods   137
Evaluation   143
Summary   144
Thought Questions   145

Chapter 8
The Ethics of Helping   147

Morality and Helping Goals   148
A Framework for Analyzing Helpers' Moral Decisions   156
Morality of Helping   159
Summary   162
Thought Questions   162

Epilogue
To Help or Not to Help   163

The Need for Helping   163
Who Will Help?   165
The Future Helper   167
In Closing   168

References   169

Suggested Readings on Helping   171

Index   175

1

A Conception of Helping

A person aspiring to become a helper is embarking on a challenging route, for helping is perhaps the most human activity possible—the compassionate extension of one person's resources to another. Probably for the very reason that helping is such an essentially human act, it is often as frustrating and discouraging as it is rewarding and exhilarating. This book will describe the ways helpers can better chart their route. This chapter will start with a more basic question, one that troubles both beginning helpers and experienced helpers alike: *What is help?* We want to say right from the start that we have no definitive answer, since helping is a continuously changing human process. Rather, we will provide some perspectives on the question. The final answer must be highly personal—you must construct your own helping philosophy.

A brief historical overview of helping is a productive place to begin.

A HISTORICAL SWEEP

A perceptive eye will see helping activity occurring everywhere. The number of formal helpers is staggering: teachers, judges, nurses, day care workers, psychologists, marriage counselors, dentists, occupational therapists, parole officers, and guidance counselors are among those engaged in helping, and the list could be easily doubled, tripled, or quadrupled. The human services offered by our society are always increasing, perhaps as human problems become increasingly complex and difficult. Never before have there been so many people engaged in helping others solve their personal problems. To understand this phenomenon, you should bear in mind one simple historical fact: helping—defined for the time being as the process of one person formally meeting with another person called the "helper" to resolve the former's life concerns—is an invention of the modern age.

Before this century, of course, people had problems. There have been marital problems since Adam and Eve, and family problems are prominent in the writings of the ancient Greeks and Romans. However, up until the end of the 19th century, these problems were handled differently than they are today. A person did not make an appointment with a marriage counselor, nor did an entire family begin family therapy. If anything, a religious leader would be consulted. In fact, most personal problems were thought of as spiritual problems, not psychological. A distressed person was considered to be not living right, or was invoking the displeasure of a deity (or The Deity), and solution of most concerns was accomplished through prayer and supplication. Extreme kinds of problem behavior would lead others to label the person "possessed" by devils and demons, and a variety of cruel and unusual treatments were available. The centrality of religion in people's lives and the power of local religious leaders exerted such a force over people's conceptions of themselves that religious frameworks provided the interpretations for almost all personal problems. (It is interesting to wonder whether people even had the notion of "personal" problems as such.) We are not arguing whether or not distressed people had or have spiritual problems but, rather, that the *social* means available to solve personal problems were religious. Priests, ministers, rabbis, and other religious people were the only helpers. (It is worth mentioning that the helping power of clergy has been recently rediscovered, as we'll discuss later.)

A transitional movement occurred during the last quarter of the 19th century, bridging the religious and social means for resolving problems. This account is derived from Smith and Zietz (1970) and from Weinberger (1969). Two related but distinct establishments took place. Settlement houses were founded and charity organization societies were begun. The first settlement house, Toynbee Hall, was founded in London by students from Cambridge University. Their interest in settling in the East London slum area was both religious and social. A two-fold goal propelled these spiritually-minded students. One goal was to learn for themselves by living in the same ways how to help the less fortunate people inhabiting the slum. The second goal was to foster greater acceptance of help by the poor and needy, largely by demonstrating the genuineness and willingness of the upper classes to be of real help without snobbery. Living in the same neighborhood was one powerful means of conveying that message. Other settlement houses rapidly came into existence. The first one in America was established by Stanton Coit in New York in the late 1880s and the most famous one, Hull House in Chicago, was founded two years later by Ellen Gates Starr and Jane Addams.

A second highlight of the transitional movement from religious to personal orientation in helping was the establishment of the Charity Organization Society, the first one founded in 1877 by Reverend F. H. Gurton in Buffalo, New York. The COS, as it was known, operated as a clearinghouse for charitable contributions from diverse organizations. Volunteers known as "friendly visitors" investigated need and gave advice to the people they were helping. The COS kept records of their investigations in order to inform the charities of eligible persons and families for distribution of funds. Gradually, the records began to demonstrate that neediness arises from causes unrelated to moral deficits, as the religious orientation had held. In addition, the records increasingly pointed to the value of taking an individualized perspective on the problems and needs of the people.

By the end of the 19th century, the landscape of the human environment had undergone a radical change. The power of scientific thinking, perhaps best seen in the Industrial Revolution and the rise of medicine, altered the ways people thought about themselves. A nonreligious understanding of people was now thought to be possible, and people began to look inward, not only upward, for guidance and knowledge. Bodies and perhaps souls *were* inherently understandable. The application of a scientific viewpoint caused a major shift in the way human problems were considered, and the notion that people were understandable in natural rather than supernatural terms was most powerfully shown by Sigmund Freud in the late 1800s.

Freud argued that distressed behavior was understandable by looking at the individual's personal circumstances, especially early experiences. His medical colleagues disagreed, taking the view that mental disease caused personal problems. The controversy over psychological vs. physiological causes for problems (especially severe ones) remains heated to this day. Nevertheless, by bringing the *psychological* nature of personal problems to the forefront, Freud set the stage for the growth of personal helping. Freud's psychoanalysis was called the "talking cure" and most of today's helpers are direct descendants of the Freudian tradition in their belief that the exchange of words— carefully selected ones, of course—is the crux of helping others.

The Freudian revolution had another long-lasting consequence: the predominance of the professional helper. Freud indeed made psychological helping into a unique profession and until recently it was thought that only help offered by highly trained professionals was of any value. Only a psychoanalyst, a psychiatrist, a psychologist, or a social worker could *really* help others. Help offered by less trained people—a minister, a friend, or a parent—was considered less valid or likely to work.

It is interesting to note that the friendly visitors, the majority of them women, increasingly requested education and training as they began to realize that the problems they encountered required more than only good will and advice. The growth of friendly visitors from nonprofessional volunteers to professional social workers was assisted by their becoming paid COS staff. The growth of professional helpers in the psychiatric and psychological fields occurred more or less simultaneously and is still ongoing.

The historical development of helping organizations has led to major problems in the present-day delivery of helping services. There are simply not enough professionals to go around while the number and complexity of personal problems are on the rise. Also, most professionals come from the middle and upper classes and relate more easily to people like themselves than to the poor. Because of this, the poorer segments of our population have been perennially underserved. These current issues are results of events that started much earlier but have culminated in a crisis in helping. The beginning question "What is help?" must once again be asked. Yet it is not by any means always the individual (or couple or family or small group) who requires change, but the social institutions surrounding us as well.

Settlement House helpers, much more than COS helpers, increasingly shifted their emphasis to social action. In many ways this is not surprising, given their programmatic social intervention for the *community* in which they resided, which often included nursery schools for the children of working parents, social clubs for young people, day camps, Americanization classes for immigrants, as well as men's groups which frequently became political forums. The helpers themselves often did social research, with the aim of demonstrating need and offering supportive data to legislatures for corrective social legislation. An outgrowth of this and related movements has been community planning and development. Community psychology, with its stress on community mental health, development, and organization, is another recent outgrowth. Thus, interventions originally aimed at individuals have been historically complemented by interventions focused on groups, communities, and social institutions. The need for all types of social intervention remains today.

To complete the brief historical backdrop, one last aspect needs to be described. We are at present in the midst of another revolution in helping, concerning the *type* of person who can help. The crux of this revolution is that nonprofessionals and paraprofessionals also can be legitimate helping agents. Some studies have shown, for example, that there are few differences between professional helpers and either those without formal training in helping (nonprofessionals) or those with some, but not extensive, training (paraprofessionals). The sheer demand for services has also forced professionals to share the work. For example, among the nonprofessionals engaging in helping others are housepersons (mostly women), retired and recently widowed people, hairdressers, and bartenders. All have been expected at one time or another to become helpers for people with whom they come in contact. Many paraprofessionals such as mental health aides, casework assistants, and teachers' aides are now taking over the roles formerly reserved for professionals. Even the medical profession has expanded its definition of helper, and much routine medical help is performed by physicians' assistants and associates.

It is appropriate to end this overview with a discussion of this radical change in the concept of helping. Helping does indeed reflect its cultural context and it is difficult to predict what the next major development in helping will be. As of now, though, there are many more people in helping roles than ever before. The types of jobs they occupy are diverse, as are their specific responsibilities to their helpees. With these issues in mind, we will try to deal with the persistent question "What is help?" If helping can be done by such a diverse group of people, its definition as "what a professional helper does" will no longer suffice.

HELPING—A DEFINITION

Helping occurs between people—the helper and the helpee. This basic idea underscores the *relationship* aspect of helping. More than one helpee can be helped by one helper at one time—for example, a family, a couple, a pair of friends, or a group of unrelated people. Community helping requires the helper(s) to develop helping relationships with many groups and individuals simultaneously. In this book, however, we'll deal with one-to-one helping relationships; the same issues and skills apply to multi-helpee relationships.

To define help entails understanding what a "helping relationship" is. We define a helping relationship as: a relationship in which two individuals are involved in resolving a concern or difficulty of one of them and/or fostering that person's personal and social development. Thus, two people are engaged in working on the concerns of one. A helping relationship is therefore not completely reciprocal; it is designed to benefit one person more than the other. It is different from a close friendship in which both people freely share whatever concerns them and eagerly give each other advice. Nor is it like two complete strangers meeting for the first time. Rather, helping is a specific kind of interaction with distinct goals—either resolving a problem or encouraging further development of some sort—that places more responsibility on the helper than might a friendship. For while a friend should be available and supportive, it is difficult for a friend to be objective. A professional helper strives to be objective and to be helpful in a directed, purposeful way.

The differentiation between helping and friendship can be illustrated from a helping relationship of one of the authors. In this case, the helpee was questioning the usefulness of the helping relationship, in that increasingly he could and did discuss the same concerns with his personal friends. Since he also discussed these concerns with the helper, he was beginning to view the helper as a friend. In the ensuing interaction between helper and helpee, the helper assisted the helpee in distinguishing similarities and differences in these relationships. For example, it became clear that the tone and process of the discussions differed. The helpee's friends listened and questioned. They gave him suggestions and offered their opinions. Clearly, they were interested in him and in *sharing* disclosures. The helper was interested in the helpee, too, but was *not* interested in sharing her concerns, except insofar as such sharing might highlight a possible goal or change a strategy. Rather, the helper gave *focused* feedback aimed at clarifying feelings, identifying contradictions, specifying goals, working out change plans, and reviewing and reinforcing behavior change. Thus, the helping relationship discouraged emotional investment in a friendship with its usual reciprocal disclosures and advice-giving. The helpee was then able to note that the value of the helping relationship for him was in the focused, objective, goal-directed feedback he received. It enabled him to not only better understand himself but also to make his own suggestions for change.

There are two major purposes of any helping relationship—remediation and enhancement. *Remediation* is the resolution of currently troubling problems; *enhancement* is the enrichment of currently nonproblematic functioning. For example, a social worker dealing with a multi-problem family is helping through remediation while the same helper conducting a parenting group for interested parents is enhancing whatever abilities parents already have. In addition, enhancement of skills serves a *preventive* function: enriching parents' skills is likely to prevent their children from developing severe problems in the future.

At the present, most of the services that helpers provide fall into the remediation category. Our human service agencies are oriented toward easing people's current pain and suffering rather than helping people to enrich their lives and thereby prevent pain and suffering in the future. Nonetheless, the opportunities for helpers to engage in enhancement services are increasing. Services like parent effectiveness training, communication skills training for couples, and assertiveness training are clearly examples of helping by enhancement. Through such training, people are helped to improve their psychosocial skills. In addition, people are helped to learn new life skills to enrich their daily living and their capacity to deal constructively with problems that arise. Helpers with a skills-training orientation can apply these strategies for remediation of helpee problems; thus, remediation and enhancement have the potential to be complementary. For example, a couple with relationship difficulties can be taught structured communication skills that will simultaneously "remediate" some of their troubles and enhance their relationship.

Whether working in a remedial or an enhancement capacity, the helper is engaged in *change*. Helpees come for help because they believe that changing their lives would alleviate distress or help them develop more comfortably. Although a helper and a helpee will occasionally decide that no change is really called for, helping at its very basic level entails addressing the issue of change. Change comes in many forms: a helpee can work on changing thoughts, feelings, actual behaviors, or some combination of these. Regardless of the type sought, change is always difficult. The helping relationship is the vehicle through which helpee change is *facilitated*.

As an example, one of the authors was engaged in a helping relationship with a person with whom it might have been easy to develop a friendship. Both helper and helpee shared a number of professional interests and an unusually large number of common acquaintances. The helper was acutely aware of the need for keeping this helping relationship on track: identifying the concerns, specifying goals for promoting the helpee's intrapersonal and interpersonal growth, and planning strategies for problem resolution and goal attainment. The helpee, on the other hand, had some difficulty. He very much wanted to shift the relationship from helper/helpee roles to friendship roles. In part, this was due to the common ground shared by the two, but even more importantly, it was because of the helpee's own difficulties with superior/subordinate relationships. Identifying the resentments he experienced in this type of relationship was helpful in specifying other related problems and then clarifying goals for change. It allowed helper and helpee alike to focus on interpersonal growth in a directed, purposeful way. It was agreed that enhancing the helpee's interpersonal communication skills and modifying his assertiveness would be a part of the change plan.

It is important to note that no helper, however well-intentioned and skilled, can *ensure* that a helpee will change. Helpees are ultimately responsible for themselves. Helpers must avoid taking the responsibility for change fully upon themselves; the final decisions belong to their helpees. In the example just given, for instance, the helpee himself had to make the commitment to change. Doing so is both attitudinal and behavioral. He had, over time, to clarify for himself just what changes he was willing to risk; then he had to act on those plans. In this case, with the facilitation of the helper, the helpee decided that he wanted to enhance his openness about feelings. He felt he had some difficulty in directly expressing his feelings about different issues with people. In particular, he avoided doing so with his parents. Helper and helpee worked out a series of steps through which the helpee gained experience in direct expression of feelings within the helping relationship as well as with his friends and his parents. Because he was willing to make some changes in his verbal behaviors, and therefore took ultimate responsibility for his change, the helpee indeed enhanced his communication skills. He was, it turned out, less able or less willing to take responsibility for changing his listening skills. Although he expressed an interest in so doing, he repeatedly failed to practice new skills. In no way could the helper do the helpee's practicing for him. The helper could and did elucidate areas of difficulty and problems with commitment to change. In addition, the helper reviewed with the helpee possible pitfalls in the change plans and assisted the helpee in modifying them. However, little change occurred at this time despite the helper's intervention because the helpee did not take responsibility for change in this area.

Another helpee, a teenager, was unhappy about being overweight. He had initially said he was interested in changing his eating behaviors. The helper was reinforcing of this, believing such change to be necessary and in the helpee's best interests. Yet after several sessions, it became clear that his commitment to the process vacillated. The helper and helpee then examined the helpee's reactions. The helpee decided he was not yet ready to give up certain habits; in essence, he decided not to make the necessary changes. The helper, of course, could not make the decision for him. Change itself is up to the helpee; the helper can only implement skills to promote changes decided and acted upon by the helpee.

PROMOTING CHANGE THROUGH HELPING: AN EQUATION

How do helpers facilitate the helpee's change? The following basic elements go into effective helping.

1. The personhood of the helper: *Helpers Are People Too*
2. Effective nonverbal behavior: *You Are What You Do*
3. Effective verbal behavior: *The Words of Helping: I. Continuing and Leading Responses*
4. Effective use of oneself: *The Words of Helping: II. Self-Referent Responses*
5. Accurate understanding of helpees: *Understanding Others' Communications*
6. Skilled use of helping processes: *Helping Strategies*
7. Sensitivity to the moral issues in helping: *The Ethics of Helping*

These elements form the framework of our book. Let's start at the top. We began this chapter by noting that helping is a "human" activity.

Because of this, the personality of the helper is important. By personhood we mean the helper's traits, attitudes, needs, motivations, and values. In other words, we are addressing those aspects of helpers that together define them as unique persons. Helpers bring themselves to helping—they cannot really do otherwise. A helper who believes that unemployed people lack drive and initiative will respond less positively to a helpee than someone who blames external economic conditions, while a helper who can see both aspects may open wider vistas for the helpee. A helper with a strong need to control may end up giving helpees excessive advice, while a helper with a high need for affection from helpees may be unable to suggest solutions to problems. Note also that helpees also react to helpers on the basis of personality. A helpee will respond differently to a quiet, gentle helper than to an assertive, outspoken one. Neither style is *necessarily* good or bad. It is worth remembering that helpees are people, too. At its most basic level, helping can be thought of as people responding to and learning from other people, as well as giving help.

In addition to their personal qualities, helpers bring skills to helping. In fact, this is what differentiates a helping interaction from an ordinary conversation. The helper makes careful use of nonverbal and verbal skills in attempting to help. Good helping also involves skillful use of oneself: in other words, the ability to discuss one's personal reactions and experiences in a constructive way. There are also more complex skills involved. Gaining an accurate and meaningful understanding of the helpee, for example, is a complicated process, but it too is a skill. So is the ability to use strategies to encourage the helpee to change. As if this weren't enough, good helping must include a concern for ethical issues. It might seem surprising to have to consider issues of right or wrong in helping others, but such issues are always present, even if not obvious. For instance, in the example given earlier where helper and helpee shared common acquaintances, the helper needed to be especially cautious about confidentiality—both about the helpee's concerns and disclosures and about the friend's knowledge and disclosures. At times, this posed a challenge but was absolutely necessary to preserve the integrity of the helping relationship.

What, then, can be expected if all of these elements are present? Assuming the helper's personhood and skills are effective, two things happen: first, a certain atmosphere is created, and second, an ongoing open and honest discussion, including consideration of plans for change, ensues. *Helping equals understanding plus action.* The atmosphere created is foremost in this equation. Helpees must come to trust their helpers. They must perceive their helpers as concerned, interested, and competent, and they must feel that their helpers respect and value them. Most helpees cannot begin to change if they are uneasy with their helpers. This is particularly true if they see their helpers as judgmental, evaluative, or critical. If helpees are on the defensive during their helping interactions, they will oppose change rather than work toward it. Defensiveness means guardedness, putting up obstacles to openness. In a facilitative helping relationship, defensiveness is minimized, largely through engendering a respectful, caring atmosphere. This can be difficult to create, and takes much work from the helper. But the *minimum* requirement for helping is that the helpee feel free to talk honestly and frankly about concerns. Helpers need to understand the helpee's life situation before they can begin to help. One helpee we have worked with had initially been seeing a different helper with whom she did not feel at ease. As a result, she failed to reveal some extremely disturbing thoughts and beliefs that would have indicated the need for a very different choice of helping strategies than had been selected. As a result, this helpee had not been able to change; her shaky trust in the helper and her lack of candor were obstacles to change that might have been modified had the helper been more fully sensitized to the effects of the atmosphere created. Unless the helper first assists the helpee to share, no change can occur.

Most helpees are reluctant *at first* to open up. Consider how you would feel if you were taking a personal problem to someone you didn't know. You'd probably be scared, not knowing what to expect. You might feel embarrassed, thinking that you shouldn't need help. You'd probably wonder how interested someone else would be. All of these are usual concerns that helpees experience; they are normal reactions to a difficult situation. How the helper relates to the helpee during their first encounter can make a tremendous difference in how the helpee feels. "Are my feelings responded to or are they ignored?" "Is the helper supportive and caring, or critical and distant?" "Is this a person I can trust?" These questions whirl through the helpee's head. If they are answered affirmatively, the helpee may be able to respond to the helper's attempts at remediation or enhancement.

Helping does not stop at the creation of an interpersonal atmosphere conducive to open and honest discussion: helping *begins* there. The helper must also work to encourage specific changes in the helpee, and it is imperative to recognize that this requires *directed* use of skills, which in turn requires an ever-expanding *knowledge base* of human behavior, development over the life span, and social systems from relationships to institutions. It is not sufficient to be very skilled, but without an adequate understanding of individual and social behavior. Nor is it sufficient to be knowledgeable about behavior but lack helping skills. Helping others is a complex, demanding task. It is our goal in this book to examine and highlight issues and means in the area of basic helping skills. We have chosen to not present the relevant knowledge base *per se,* for that is the task of other books—and especially the task of each individual helper. It is the helper's responsibility to select experiences and do reading that will develop helping capacities and promote increasingly skillful facilitation of the helping process.

THE HELPING PROCESS

Helping involves exploration of issues, decisions regarding change, and action for change. The helping process occurs in several stages, stages which may be reinitiated if necessary in order to confront and act on all the issues a helpee may face. We see these stages as follows:

1. Entry
2. Initial Exploration
3. Clarification
4. Integration
5. Program Planning
6. Action-Taking
7. Reviewing
8. Terminating

For the helper to assist the helpee to make specific changes in thinking or behavior, the helper must proceed in stages. *Entry* is the first stage, and it is during this stage that the atmosphere is first created. The helpee is helped to enter into the helping relationship. The helper defines the relationship by exploring the helpee's own expectations and by suggesting realistic ones. Some structure for the helping interactions may be suggested as well.

The next three stages further promote an atmosphere conducive to change and examine the need and direction of that change. Stage 2, *Initial Exploration,* involves encouraging the helpee to share concerns and exploring what feelings the helpee recognizes as basic to those concerns. Why does the helpee need help? How does the helpee wish to be enhanced? How does the helpee feel about current problems? *Exploration* is the key word. Stage 3, *Clarification,* involves further examination of the concerns or needs, and seeks to clarify the deeper implicit and explicit feelings of the helpee. At this stage, the helper strives to identify as yet unnoticed issues that play roles in the helpee's problems or concerns and to discover how these issues are affecting the helpee. Further, the helper strives to identify the *themes* present in the helpee's thinking and behavior which, *if weaknesses,* contribute to the continuation of the problems or, *if strengths,* may contribute to the alleviation of the problems. Patterns of feelings, thoughts, and actions are brought to awareness in Stage 3. In Stage 4, *Integration,* the helper is involved in assisting the helpee to pull together the information gathered up to this point, in order to make decisions regarding goals for actions. Setting goals is perhaps the essential aspect of this stage.

The three following stages encourage the helpee to act on insights and new awarenesses. *Action* is the goal of this part of the helping process, action that follows the helper's understanding of the helpee's situation. Much time is spent in working on the specifics of action for change. It is a mistake to assume, for example, that as soon as helpees are aware of their problem and their feelings about it, they will automatically change. The helper must, *in some sense,* share with the helpee the responsibility for change. Both work on the process together in Stages 5, 6, and 7. Stage 5, *Program Planning,* involves assisting the helpee in specifying an action plan to meet the goals set earlier. The helper draws upon knowledge of change strategies and human behavior to guide the helpee in planning how to make changes. This knowledge is also drawn on in Stage 6, *Action-Taking,* when the helper helps the helpee to carry out the planned program for change. In some instances, the helper will simply suggest possible change methods which the helpee must carry out. Assigning "homework" is one example, where the helpee is encouraged to do certain things outside of the helping relationship, such as initiating one new relationship during the week or practicing honest communication with one's spouse. In other instances, the helper is directly involved in the action, in that much of it takes place *during* the helping interaction: rehearsing with the helpee how to go about initiating a relationship or how to communicate honestly. It should be noted that in either case, the helper at this stage must actively reinforce positive steps—however small—toward reaching the agreed-upon goals. Also, the helper may be involved in giving feedback to the helpee about how the plan is progressing and how the helpee is changing. Stage 7, *Reviewing,* is simply that the helper assists the helpee in reviewing the goals, their association and relevance to the problems identified, and the current outcome of the change program. The purposes are to gauge the need for further work and to rework or set up a new series of steps toward specific change.

If helpee and helper are satisfied that the goals have been met, Stage 8 has probably been reached: *Termination.* Terminating the helping relationship involves taking stock of current resources and strengths and how they may further bolster the helpee's *own* goal setting and attainment in the future. While closing the relationship is often difficult for both helper and helpee who may have formed strong attachments, good helping results in helpees' being in charge of their own lives and knowing how to make and carry out life decisions on their own. Although early in the helping relationship the helpers may feel that they are "in charge," this is really only a temporary state of affairs. Good helping is designed to make the helper obsolete.

SUMMARY: "WHAT IS HELP?" REVISITED

Helping is, therefore, a process. It is the careful use of both personal traits and characteristics and of helping skills and knowledge to create a relationship that encourages the helpee to consider what, if any, changes would be beneficial. Helping, then, is not confined to a specific group. There are formal helpers whose prime occupation is to work with others; they may be professionals or, more and more frequently, paraprofessionals. Helping also occurs in nonprofessional contexts. Such informal helping as done by a concerned minister, an ambulance driver, a close friend, or a relative is every bit as legitimate a form of helping. If a person is conscientiously using certain words and avoiding others; being accepting while someone else talks or seeking a real understanding of the concern and not haphazardly offering advice; encouraging another to become more capable of resolving certain concerns in the future—then this person is *helping*. A person sitting in a "helping office" who does not do these things is *not* helping, regardless of training or prestige. Workers in the human services are becoming increasingly aware that helpers can be found in many places and that there is much untapped helping potential in our communities.

A FINAL NOTE

The remainder of this book describes the elements of the helping process listed earlier. We take a *skills approach* to helping, which assumes that helpers are made, not born. We further assume that people, whether formally or informally involved with others, can enhance their helping skills and be more effective in dealing with helpees. (We also take an *enhancement approach!*) Too often books on helping present theoretical models without pointing out what helpers must *say* and *do* to help. We noted earlier that theories of helping are clearly important, yet our purpose in this book is not to summarize others' theories. Rather, we hope to describe the ingredients of a good recipe for helping. We are, in essence, detailing the helping equation presented earlier. We don't believe that reading this book is enough to become a good helper; extensive practice is also called for. However, we hope to sensitize the reader to the skills and competencies of basic helping. We also intend to broaden your perspective so that you can think about the ethical questions involved in helping others. The conception of helping taken in the rest of the book is one we find particularly useful. We hope it makes the navigation easier for you as well.

THOUGHT QUESTIONS

1. How does helping differ from a friendship?
2. Who is responsible for change in a helping relationship?
3. How might a friend be more helpful than a professional helper?
4. Is a helper a director or a facilitator? Why?
5. How can the helper overcome the helpee's initial reluctance to share important problems?
6. Which stages of the helping relationship do you expect to be especially difficult?
7. Which stages of the helping relationship do you expect to be especially easy?
8. How does remediation differ from enhancement?
9. Why do helpees have problems?
10. Why do helpers help?

2

Helpers Are People Too

There are many ways in which a helper has a profound influence on a helping relationship. The technical skills the helper brings to the relationship will certainly affect the outcome; for example, a capable helper must know how to comfort a suddenly widowed person. In addition, the helper's personal view of what constitutes help may alter the nature of the relationship. A helper who believes people should "make it" on their own will respond differently from a helper with another viewpoint. Finally, the helper brings a unique constellation of needs and motivations to the helping interaction. Some have suggested that this latter factor, the helper's personality or "person," is *the* crucial influence in the helping process. As Kell and Mueller (1966) state:

> The counselor, as in any other occupation, has primarily himself to bring to the helping relationship. He may learn of technical aids such as tests; he may learn interviewing techniques; he may read widely and copiously about people; he may search desperately for a philosophy or orientation; he may even attempt to copy the behaviors of those who are regarded as experts. Yet, ultimately, what he brings to his encounters with his clients is himself [p. 65].

The uniqueness that each helper brings to his or her work is an intrinsic part of the human exchange of helping. Consider the helper's intention in this interaction:

Helpee: I don't know what to do. My boss still won't give me a raise.
Helper: Well, it seems obvious that you haven't really asked her in the right way.
Helpee: What do you mean, right way?

16   CHAPTER 2

> Helper: You know what I mean.
> Helpee: No I don't, really!
> Helper: Well, give her an ultimatum—either I get the raise or I go. Be decisive. Don't beat around the bush!
> Helpee: But she may fire me.
> Helper: Well, that's a risk you take.

This helper is being quite directive and is proceeding to resolve the helpee's problem in a certain way. But why is the helper so invested in this particular solution? It may well be the "best" solution, so the helper may be justified in pushing for it; on the other hand, this particular helper may have a very strong need to control events and may be imposing this on the helpee. In some situations, a strong need for control can be very useful for a helper to express since it may lead to helpee change; in other situations, it may simply lead the helper to "take over" the helpee's life.

It is difficult to understand how the helper *as a person* influences the helping process. In the past, therapists were expected to enter psychotherapy themselves to resolve conflicts in their own lives. More recently, counselors have begun to engage in personal awareness groups in which they could discuss personal concerns with one another. Regardless of the method used, it is vital for helpers to "know themselves." In this chapter, we will attempt to answer several questions about this process of looking inward: What should a helper study about himself or herself? How can the helper do this? What real difference in helping will result?

We believe that helpers must know *how* their needs, motivations, and values *relate specifically to why they choose to help*. While it is important to know as much about oneself as possible, the energy and time expended on a *general* understanding of oneself may be unrealistic and even impossible. Further, it is possible that seeking a general understanding may inhibit the helper's effectiveness since it may lead to over-analysis of behavior. There is a fine line distinguishing a productive examination of oneself from an overly analytic examination. In this chapter we will focus on a limited self-examination of one's needs, motivations, and beliefs in the context of helping.

NEEDS

Why Do We Help?

Many people in the helping professions, when asked why they chose their particular career, would reply "Because I like to help people." If pressed further, some might refer to the generally troubled times and the interest in helping others "cope." Others might mention a valuable experience they once had with another person—perhaps a minister or a guidance counselor—and say that they'd like to provide such help to others. Basically, however, these are *reasons* for helping. They do not concern the personality of the helper or how the helper's unique set of needs and motivations led to choosing a helping career.

To commit oneself to a career is a major event, and it reflects one's personality to a great degree. The helper's needs and motives must be considered to understand the commitment. Motivation can be analyzed in a variety of ways: analyzing the needs the helper fulfills for himself or herself in helping others is one important way. This will help to explain why one person chooses to become a counselor in prisons instead of a guard, or a nurse instead of a medical technician, or a clinician instead of a researcher.

In any relationship, helping or otherwise, an exchange between the two people involved is taking place. In other words, either implicitly or explicitly the helper and helpee are working out an agreement: "If I give you this, you will give me that." The exchange is usually not in terms of tangible items like money; it can be the exchange of respect for caring, of status for information, or of gossip for advice. Most helpers exchange their expertise for their helpees' respect. Some exchange their experience for being looked up to by their helpees. Others, though unaware of it, provide help so that their helpees will provide them with companionship. Helpers, because of their needs, can strongly control the nature or direction of the helping interaction. For example, a helping relationship could be perpetuated not for exploration or solutions of stated goals but because both helper and helpee are lonely, isolated people.

Helpers' needs may be manifested in very specific ways in helping. For example, because of personal needs a helper may become more interested in a helpee's sexual fantasies than in the helpee's problems in holding a job. Another helper may be unable to listen to a client who holds unconventional attitudes about marriage. A helper who fears hostility may not listen to an angry helpee since it is too personally threatening, or a helper with a pessimistic outlook on life might be unresponsive to a helpee's hopefulness.

One of the authors recalls an experience with a woman client close to her own age. The helper found this particular person very interesting and very satisfying to work with. The young woman was very verbal and quite willing to explore her needs, beliefs, and typical patterns of response and was able to open herself up to some necessary risk-taking in order to make agreed upon changes.

As this helping relationship progressed, it became clear to the helper that some of her own needs were involved in how she viewed and planned for progress in the relationship. Two needs in particular stood out: one was a need for a greatly satisfying intellectual and emotional work-out, which this relationship was providing; the other was a need for emotional closeness and intimacy, particularly in woman-to-woman relationships. Both needs tended to make the helper wish that the relationship would continue for an indefinite, lengthy time. How did these needs and wishes affect her helping behaviors? At times, the helper found herself postponing discussion of an important issue. At other times, she realized that she was not discouraging the client from going on tangents. As she recognized these influences, the helper modified her own behaviors, while remaining acutely aware of a special liking for and ease with this helpee that did not permeate other helping relationships.

Thus, help meets the needs of the helper and helpee alike. This does not assume, however, that helpers don't want to help others or that their reasons are selfish ones. It does imply that what we do for others, we do, in part, *for ourselves*—and that what we are doing for ourselves can at times interfere with what we are trying to do for others.

Many helpers fail to understand how their own needs may interfere with, as well as generally influence, effective helping, particularly if they view "good" helpers as purely altruistic and only concerned with their helpees' welfare. It is difficult for beginning helpers to grasp how fulfillment of the helper's needs can occur, since the purpose of the relationship is to help the helpee. But helping, like any other career, must be rewarding to the helper, and this means that personal needs of various kinds are being met. If helping is not personally rewarding, there is no reason for a counselor, teacher, or other helper to continue helping. Helpers frequently say that their reward is seeing the change that takes place in their helpees. Yet this must entail a great deal more frustration than satisfaction, since few helpees show the kinds of changes that would be gratifying for the helper. There are usually other rewards aside from helpee success that motivate the helper.

Kinds of Helpers' Needs

Since the purpose of a helping relationship is to benefit the helpee, the specific needs a helper has are not often considered. Yet through the helper role, the helper's personal needs are often fulfilled. These needs include a need to control, a need to nurture, a need for affection, and needs which relate to personal anxieties and conflicts. How can such needs negatively and positively affect the helping process?

Some helpers may use the helping relationship to meet their needs for power, prestige, and control. After all, the helper is in a position of power since the helpee comes at times of distress. Helpers may evoke the mystique and mystery of helping relationships by trying to impress the helpee with their interpretations or their sensitivity. Physicians too often fall into the power trap, a negative aspect of the need to control. Playing expert is important to many of them, and unfortunately it often leads to ignoring the feelings of their patients. An obstetrician we are acquainted with often infuriates women by refusing to answer their questions and saying "Leave it to me. I'll decide what's best." This helper wrests control by denying legitimacy to the helpee's concerns and by evoking medical mystique. On the positive side, having a strong need for control may benefit the helpee by offering a model of assuming responsibility and self-direction in one's life. In one helping relationship, one of the authors facilitated this type of learning in a graduate student who had been increasingly indecisive as family pressure and disapproval about her academic career mounted. Part of the learning process involved modeling decision-making skills by the helper, who took great care not to make or become entangled in making decisions. For the helpee, "I'm leaving the decisions up to you" was the clear and direct message.

The need to nurture helpees may take several forms. Some helpers need love and acceptance from their helpees. To attain this, they may cultivate helpee dependency, which can make the helper feel even more important but which can also foster undue reliance on the helper. In some helping relationships we have observed, the helpers seemed to have become enmeshed in the day-to-day living of the helpees involved. Rather than attempting to resolve problems independently, the helpees tended to call upon their helpers. Thus, phone calls to quash a family argument between uncle and mother, to intervene in a bureaucratic decision about schooling, to arrange for the receipt of additional monies from a governmental agency, or to write letters of recommendation for jobs or college were common daily occurrences among this group. Another problematic influence of the need to nurture and be loved in return may be seen in the helper's avoiding confronting a helpee so the helpee will not turn on her or him in anger. As a means of self-protection, the helper may actually be of little help to the helpee who poses a threat to the helper's own feelings of security and adequacy.

Positive influences of the need to nurture include promoting a sense of being cared about in the helpee. Many helpees feel quite alone and unloved. Helping them experience warmth in an interpersonal relationship is one aspect of helping them learn new patterns of responses. Another positive influence of this need is the sense of both the helper and the helpee that the helper can be counted on. Sometimes helpees test this dependability, for example, by creating crises to which they observe the helper's response. A rather extreme example is that of a helpee who becomes very depressed sometimes between scheduled sessions. Calling the helper to discuss this, the helpee is interested in just how caring the helper is, whether or not the helper is willing to go out of the way for the helpee, and so on. Early in the helping relationship, a nurturant helper is likely to be willing to talk with the helpee sooner than the originally scheduled time. The helpee gets the feeling, then, that this helper cares and is willing to rearrange things to be of help.

Another nurturant need, particularly important for male helpers, is the need to give tenderness and caring to another person. Being tender and sharing feelings are socially defined in our society as feminine traits and are often deemed inappropriate for males. However, a male helper may use the helping relationship as a safe way to give tenderness and share feelings. Again, positive effects on the helping relationships may include the helpee's feeling warmly cared about and important to another person. For the helper, such a need may allow him (or her) to be open to many different types of people and to invite their trust. This then can make for flexibility in helping. More negatively, nurturance as a need to be needed may lead to the helper's extending dependency on the part of the helpee. A dependent helpee provides an immediate reward for the helper in that those needs are gratified through the helpee's dependent behavior. A helper with a strong need to be needed in a nurturing role may extend the helping relationship too long. Similarly, the counselor's ambivalence about adequacy and power may also be involved in nurturing the helpee; that is, a dependent helpee affords the counselor more control and power in the relationship.

Another set of helper needs are those which relate to personal conflicts. For example, a rebellious helper might find it easier to be supportive of a helpee's nonconformity to societal norms than to openly be a rebel; being in the helping position is a much more acceptable way to express that rebellion. This may have some positive influences. A helper who is philosophically committed to racial equality may strongly encourage helpees to assert themselves in relevant situations. Some counselors, for example, argue that Black helpees often feel powerless and out of control but may be helped by being encouraged to assert power. Teaching assertiveness skills may be another aspect of the helper's role here, assisted by the helper's own needs to be nonconforming. Yet the very same philosophical commitment may negatively influence helping. If the helper models outrage and hostility in the guise of assertion, the helpee may be learning counterproductive approaches to power and change. Different helpers have different personal conflicts, and thus the variety of personal conflict needs which could be met through helping are great.

Although we have focused on what the helper does to meet his or her needs, the helping process involves at least two people. In part, the helpee contributes to the helper meeting his or her own needs—sometimes at the helpee's expense and usually as a function of the helper's personal conflicts. In a way, it may be said that helper and helpee are engaged in a kind of game-playing. Eric Berne, in his book *Games People Play* (1964), identified several such games that helpers play in helping relationships. A helper playing a game called "I'm only trying to help you" seems to be an altruistic good samaritan who will offer solicitous, caring aid in crisis. However, this person basically expects the help to be of no avail, mainly due to an unstated feeling that people are disappointing. In an extreme case, a teacher may offer to tutor a pupil after class and may spend a lot of time working with that student individually while setting both of them up to be disappointed and unsatisfied by presenting such difficult tasks or problems that the student has no way of succeeding. A helper who plays the game Berne called "Indigent" may seem interested in the helpee's welfare and self-reliance, but ultimately keeps the helpee dependent. Berne described a social worker whose behavior actually resulted in maintaining the helpee's impoverished dependence on her and various agencies. Lastly, a helper playing "Psychiatry" seemingly offers to help a helpee work out problems in mutual collaboration, but actually keeps the client in awe of his or her expertise. The underlying theme in each of the games is the helper's pursuit of personal goals in helping. Clarification of these implicit "rules of the game" involves some understanding of the helper's motivation and values.

The Importance of Understanding One's Needs in Helping Relationships

The helper needs to be aware of his or her unique needs since some may interfere with the helping process. However, while some may interfere, it does not follow that there are "good" and "bad" needs. Knowledge of one's needs as a helper serves to maintain direction over one's helping. Which needs interfere and which facilitate your helping others? And *how* do they do so?

It is not being suggested that people who have "selfish" needs should not act as helpers. People must have their basic needs fulfilled to do anything well, and selfishness may well be an essential ingredient in helping. *Needs* are neither facilitating nor debilitating to the helping relationship; rather, helper *behaviors* which reflect needs can facilitate or work against the helping process. For example, take the need for control. For one helper this need may be very powerful and negatively influential in actual helping situations: the helper may give much advice, may question the helpee's own solutions, and be critical of other alternatives. Another helper who may be aware of a need for control would be very cautious about advice and try to listen very carefully to the helpee's ideas. The important point is the way a helper's needs are manifested in actual helping. One cannot suddenly stop having a personal need, but it is very possible to be aware of the need's influence on what you actually say and do.

What actual *difference* does the understanding of one's needs make? In a helping relationship, it is likely that a helper's needs, motivations, and values will emerge in subtle ways. A helper must be aware of them to monitor his or her own behavior. The task of the helper is to discover not only what his or her needs are but also what he or she does to fulfill them. Thus, the major advantage for the helper in having self-knowledge is that it helps to maintain control of the helping relationship. Maintaining control of the process of helping includes assuring that one's own values, needs, and interests are not interfering with those of the helpee.

Another extremely valuable effect of understanding one's own needs has to do with modeling and experience. Helpers can work more effectively toward helpee goals if they know their own personal goals because they have experienced the very process of exploration which they expect of their helpees. The perceptive helper can check for distortions and difficulties caused by his or her own needs and can understand why undue time is given to certain aspects of the helpee's problem, or why it seems preferable to hear only certain kinds of concerns, and can work to change this. In addition, dependence on helpees for need fulfillment can be decreased, while the helper's own personal relationships can be more fully developed. Maintaining a relationship with a person who profusely offers praise may reflect the helper's need for approval. Recognizing that the relationship has been continued in order to fulfill this need and not really to further the helpee's goals is an important first step in altering the relationship. Thus, understanding of one's own motivations allows the helper to plan more during helping. Before you enter a helping relationship, then, ask yourself the following.

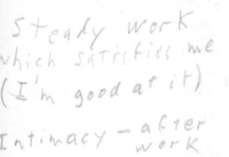

1. What are my own personal needs that seek fulfillment?
2. In what ways will I use the helping relationship to satisfy these needs?
3. How can I either meet these needs in more constructive ways or set them aside during the helping relationship so they do not inhibit the growth of the helpee?

A Process of Identifying One's Needs

As you try to answer these questions it will be helpful to have some guidelines to identify your needs. First, what is a need? A need is an emotional state in which something is necessary, desirable, required, or wanted. It may be a wish for something lacking or desired. Maslow's

(1968) conception of needs is useful here. He defines several categories of needs: physiological needs, safety needs, love and belongingness needs, esteem needs, and self-actualization needs. Some examples are given below.

1. *Physiological Needs*
   - food
   - sex drive
   - water
   - homeostatic maintenance
   - sleep
   - money (to make a living)
2. *Safety Needs*
   - safety from threat or danger
   - fear of loss of parent or object
   - fear of a new situation or new people, the unfamiliar
   - preference for the familiar and known rather than the unknown
   - fear of impending danger or catastrophe
   - predictability of the future
3. *Love and Belonging Needs*
   - love, affection, belong, be a part of, mothering
   - intimacy, interaction, giving love, nurturance
   - closeness, acceptance, receiving love, protection
   - like me, acknowledgement, to be needed
   - negatives—loneliness, outsider, isolated
4. *Esteem Needs*
   - self-respect, self-esteem, self-confidence
   - to be needed, superiority, accomplishment
   - independence, achievement, adequacy
   - dominance, self-worth, to be useful
   - appreciated, prestige, status
   - recognition, attention, importance
   - negatives—inadequacy, inferiority, incompetence, low self-esteem, lack of confidence
5. *Self-Actualization Needs*
   - to be most capable of, personal growth
   - challenge, variety
   - interesting vs. boring, self-introspection

After you have determined that what you thought was a need is in fact a need, then you are able to examine how and if you presently seek its fulfillment by helping. If you are fulfilling it within a helping relationship, how is it influencing the relationship? Is it interfering with helpee growth? How? If so, how can you set aside these needs during the helping process? Is it providing any positive benefits? How? If so, how can you enhance the positive impact?

The Development of One's Needs

As helpers learn to examine their needs, there is a tendency for them to assume that once needs are examined, considered, and "set aside" from the helping relationship, the process is complete. On the contrary, the more one examines needs, the more one understands them. With increased experience in helping others, helpers start to understand and identify more explicitly their needs as well as identify new needs that they have. Thus, understanding one's needs is a continual process.

One helper, during her initial training, identified the following needs to be a helper:

1. *A need for self-respect:* "I want and need to view myself with a high degree of esteem."
2. *A need for respect from others:* "I have a need for recognition, for being looked up to."
3. *A need to be needed:* "I need for people to depend on me in a number of ways. I'll always be needed as a helper in helping relationships."

Later on, as she extended her training, she expanded on her needs in this way:

1. *A need to be useful:* "My strongest need is my need to be useful, to be doing something worthwhile and valuable, something I am capable of. In helping, I'm finding a sense of accomplishment in being challenged. It is increasingly a feeling of being productive and meaningful, benefiting both myself and others."
2. *A need for recognition:* "I desire status. I not only want to be appreciated, I need to be seen as important and as doing something commendable and worthy of recognition. I also realize there is some sense of superiority in the helper role, and that is a part of status. I need to feel special. I suppose this enhances my own feelings of esteem."
3. *A need for closeness:* "I need a feeling of trust and of being trusted. In helping, the helpee reveals her or his real self and feelings. It takes this trust to be able to open up. I find I like and need this intimacy. Part of my feeling fulfilled is in feeling close, trusted, and intimate. I know I seek it in personal relationships, but I recognize this need for closeness even more than needing to be needed as something I seek in choosing to help others."

Thus, this helper continued to explore and reflect on her needs as she grew in her field and was better able to express her needs as she progressed. She was also better able to identify more complex aspects of those needs and new perspectives on some of them. This was useful to her in examining how her needs were positively and negatively influencing her helping interactions and in enabling her to modify some of her helping behaviors.

It is not only the expanded understanding of one's needs that makes a continual examination a necessity. It is also the fact that a helper's needs are constantly changing. As we develop, new needs may arise and old needs may disappear; some needs may get stronger and others weaker. The changing nature of one's needs may even lead to a reconsideration of the decision to be a helper. If needs change, so might vocational or career interests. A careful examination of needs may influence a person to decide that these needs cannot be met through helping, that they were once being met through helping but are not now, or that they can be met through helping without interfering with the helping process. This process of self-exploration and discovery is basic to remaining an effective helper.

Following graduate school, one of the authors became a counseling psychologist at a university counseling center. At that time, counseling met a number of his needs. He enjoyed establishing relationships and getting to know people more or less one at a time (need for belongingness). He enjoyed having people dependent on him, valuing his suggestions for changing their behavior and impressed with his ability to help them (need for self-esteem). Hopefully, these needs were being met without interfering with the process of counseling. However, during the subsequent six to eight years, his needs changed. His original needs were no longer as strong; he became concerned with whether he was capable of transmitting his ideas to others; his focus became more internally directed (self-actualization need). Further, he was unsatisfied with the respect and valuing of several individuals. He wanted to be respected and achieve professionally within the larger community of professional psychologists rather than within a purely helping relationship (need for others' esteem). As he recognized these changing needs, his activities began to change. These changes eventually culminated in his leaving the counseling position and taking an academic position where his changing needs could be met.

The career history described above was not *totally* a result of changing needs. Yet the fact that the needs did change contributed to the career shift. As needs change, understanding of one's needs will increase and this will affect one's behavior. Therefore, we must conscientiously and continuously monitor our needs as they relate to helping.

BELIEFS AND VALUES

Needs versus Beliefs and Values

During the first section of this chapter, we focused on the needs a helper brings to a helping relationship. In this section we will focus on the values and beliefs of helpers. Needs, beliefs, and values are directly or indirectly inferred from one's behavior; however, a need is motivated from within, while values and beliefs are derived from one's attitudes about others. In other words, beliefs or values are the consequence of one's world view. Our beliefs and values, both of which are a set of attitudes, affect our helping and so must be considered.

What Are Beliefs and Values?

No two world views are the same. From parents, peers, and significant others, we have developed attitudes about a wide variety of subjects. Most of these values are not explicit—we are not aware of their influence. Nevertheless, they have certain impacts on our helping behavior, so we need to examine them and their consequences.

One of the most general sets of beliefs are our attitudes about the nature of people. More specifically, do we believe people have free will or are they determined? Are people rational or irrational? Are they good, bad, or neutral in terms of basic nature? While these questions may appear to be quite abstract, they make a real difference. For example, a helper who believes helpees to be good, rational, and to have free will would respond and have very different expectations about the helping process than would a helper who has opposite beliefs. The two helpers would differ on the relative importance of the circumstances, on how accurate the helpee would be in assessing his or her own problems, on how much change is possible. Further, the two would differ on the role the helper should play.

In addition to general beliefs about the nature of people, helpers also have values about specific current controversial issues like abortion, suicide, homosexuality, political activism, women's liberation, and a variety of other subjects. These values will also enter the helping relationship. When a helper sees a helpee experiencing a problem relating to the helper's values, the helper is in conflict. Should the helper avoid influencing the helpee toward his or her own position? Is it possible not to influence a helpee? Should the helper specifically try to influence the decision without the helpee knowing, or should he or she indicate a position on the subject?

While helpers may be aware of the value conflicts they encounter, they are less aware of the impact their values have on the helping relationship. Consider the following situation.

As a community counselor, you are often called upon to do group counseling in the community. During one month, you are called to counsel several groups of adolescent girls. The leader of the first group says that her girls, aged 13-15, are interested in preparing for careers as well as marriage and want to be prepared psychologically, vocationally, and behaviorally for both. Her girls concur with the leader's assessment of their needs. The leader of the second group, again with group concurrence, states that her girls want to prepare for lives as better mothers and wives. They see a career orientation as inappropriate for women and feel that a woman's place is in the home helping her husband and children to achieve in the best way possible. The third leader, with group approval, states that their group is interested in preparing for a career without marriage and want assistance to combat other's attempts to induce them to marry. Marriage to them is equivalent to serfdom.

Will you help all three groups? Is your strategy going to be the same? How will your values enter into the helping?

At some point in many helping relationships, you will have a value conflict. It can be as obvious as the example just presented, but often it will be so subtle the conflict will not be evident until you look back on the situation. As with personal needs, values must be known. Helpers must be aware of how their values enter their helping so that they do not hinder the process. This will be considered further in Chapter 8, "The Ethics of Helping."

SUMMARY

Helpers are people, for better or worse. People's motives, needs, attitudes, and values always enter into their dealings with others, and this is true of the helping situations, too. However, a helper has a greater responsibility than other people to be aware of the impact of his or her needs, attitudes, and values. The more helpers know about themselves, the more likely that their needs, beliefs, and values will not interfere with helpees' progress—and the more likely it is that their needs and beliefs will be positively directed. If a helper has very strong values and beliefs, it is often most beneficial to share them with the helpee—in essence, "to put them on the table." In this way, the helpee has the chance to reject or to accept them outright. If they influence the helpee, it is then with his or her willingness. Even this, however, is still a question: What values or beliefs should a helper "put on the table"? When is it appropriate to do so? Are there other approaches to strong beliefs which may be helpful? Recognizing the needs, beliefs, and values is the first stage. Recognizing their influence and deciding on appropriate behaviors follow from it.

THOUGHT QUESTIONS

1. How might you discover your own needs?
2. What past experiences led you to a helping career?
3. How would you feel if a helpee rejected you?
4. How would you respond if a helpee described you as a lifesaver?
5. How have your needs changed in the last two years?
6. What kinds of helpees would be hard for you to help?
7. What kinds of helpees would you really enjoy helping?
8. On what issues do you hold very strong opinions? How might these positions interfere with helping?
9. What would you consider to be the *worst* possible experience you could have with a helpee?
10. What would you consider to be the *best* possible experience you could have with a helpee?

3

You Are What You Do: Nonverbal Behavior in Helping

One researcher has estimated that only about 7% of the meaning of our communication to others is based on the words we say (Mehrabian, 1968). We tell others what we mean by nonverbal cues like our tone of voice, our facial expressions, and our sensitivity to nonverbal messages. A person about to begin a new job may tell a helper how he is looking forward to starting, while his facial expression says "I'm really scared. I've never held a job so demanding before. Will I make it?" A sensitive helper will be alert to these feelings and discuss his or her perceptions with the helpee.

At its best, helping is a sharing process. The helpee must be willing to discuss thoughts and feelings that may be distressing and confusing. The helper must be willing to listen to these concerns and attempt to facilitate the helpee's exploration and solution of them. Most helpers intend to communicate this willingness. Whether or not they succeed depends largely on their own nonverbal communication. Simply put, does the helper's nonverbal behavior communicate sincerity in an opening remark such as "How can I be of help?" Or does a bored facial expression, slumped posture, curtness, or distractability tell a different story?

Sensitivity to nonverbal behavior is a two-way process. The helper must be aware of his or her *own* nonverbal behavior as well as that of the helpee—because *both* are communicating nonverbally. The helper, however, must direct nonverbal behavior so that an effective helping relationship can best develop.

Nonverbal communication is a language of its own, and specific nonverbal behaviors are the vocabulary. The helper must speak this language fluently to allow minimal confusion in what is "said" nonverbally to the helpee. Just as people differ in their verbal clarity, so do they in their nonverbal clarity.

This chapter will acquaint the reader with the language of nonverbal communication and its role in helping. We'll first discuss the interpersonal importance of nonverbal behavior. Then we'll discuss the ways in which verbal and nonverbal cues relate to each other. Finally, we'll present guidelines for effective use of nonverbal behavior in helping others.

WHAT SHOULD BE COMMUNICATED NONVERBALLY?

A personal example: one of the authors, not known for courage in the face of medical procedures like blood tests, had to have two tests done in one day by two sets of nurses. Feeling slightly nervous already, he entered the first office to find two nurses chatting about their husbands. They didn't turn around and he got their attention only with an exasperated (and loud) "Excuse me!" Finally one nurse turned toward him, begrudgingly took his name, and curtly told him to take a seat. No smile, little eye contact, nothing conveying the slightest personal interest. The blood was drawn. He felt like a laboratory animal.

The second test was completely different, not in the actual procedures but in his feelings before and after. This is what happened: in the second office, he was greeted by a cheerful nurse with a warm smile. Her voice was personable and "nonofficial." She leaned forward, looked at him, even got out of her chair, and he, in turn, felt more relaxed and more prepared for what was to come. He felt he was being treated as a person rather than an object, and the difference was clearly in this nurse's nonverbal behavior. In the first situation, a message of distinct disinterest was sent; in the second, a message of personal involvement was warmly conveyed.

We're all very sensitive to nonverbal behavior. Indeed, we read others' "real" intent by attending to their nonverbal communication. What is the *helper's* intent in using nonverbal behavior? What should his or her communication be? The following are important uses of nonverbal behavior in helping:

1. to listen to the helpee;
2. to convey "with-ness" to the helpee;
3. to encourage further helpee exploration and discussion;
4. to reinforce the helpee.

Listening

The effective helper clearly conveys that he or she is interested in the helpee. In large part, this interest is conveyed through nonverbal listening behaviors, sincerely but deliberately modulated so that the helpee feels the helper's genuine concern. Basically, the nonverbally created impression must be that of an actively concerned *listener* who is completely focused on understanding. The essential message is "Yes, I do want to listen to what's on your mind. What you're saying right now is very important to me. I will not be distracted from focusing right on *you*."

Most of you as helpers naturally convey this message. You will move your chair closer to the helpee, look directly at the helpee, and smile when a smile is appropriate. In other words, you will be closely attentive. These behaviors and others comprise *nonverbal attending behavior*. Unfortunately, some helpers will say "Tell me how I can be of help" verbally but proceed nonverbally to withdraw the offer by not leaning forward, not maintaining eye contact, and so on. Effective helpers must make deliberate use of the self—here, *nonverbally*—and must be alert to the messages they convey to ensure the reception of the vital messages. They do not allow their nonverbal attending behavior to express or even imply a lack of interest and attentiveness. Have you had the experience of talking with a friend who persists in looking around at others while you talk? You probably felt "Why bother? She or he isn't listening." Yet your friend may have believed she or he was listening even though you didn't.

In addition to making the helpee feel comfortable, focused nonverbal attending behavior serves a purpose for the helper as well by making it easier to actively listen to the helpee. If you are facing someone and looking at him or her directly, it is difficult *not* to hear what that person is saying. The helper in an important sense deliberately screens distractions in order to better develop a complete understanding of the helpee's nonverbal and verbal behavior.

Even if the helper is not yet deeply interested in a particular person, interest and concern should clearly be conveyed. Helpers are ethically obligated to respect each helpee they come in contact with as a human being. Demonstrating interest through focused nonverbal attending behavior is one basic way to do so. Furthermore, we often find that we become interested through acting interested. It is important to clarify this point: we clearly do not suggest deception but, rather, deliberate helping behaviors intentionally employed by a sincere helper who is eager to help to the best of his or her abilities. A relevant example is brought to mind. One of the authors was contacted by a helpee regarding marital relationship counseling. The first phone conversation, however, took place after this helpee had already made an appointment with another helper. During the conversation, the helpee asked the author to find the address and phone number of the helper with whom she had made the previous appointment; she had lost the information. The author did so, and was then asked to call this other helper to confirm the appointment and make certain of the address. The author declined to do so, suggesting that this was the helpee's responsibility. Thinking this contact would be the only contact between them, the author was surprised to hear again from this helpee. Rather than telephoning, however, the helpee arrived at the office without an appointment, long before office hours began. The author had a choice: speak with the woman or inform her that it was impossible to meet without an appointment. The author chose to speak with her, responding to the anxiety and worry she had conveyed previously over the phone and now by appearing at the office in this manner. While the author felt ethically obliged to assist the person in distress, she simultaneously felt quite annoyed by this individual's style of approach and was also distanced by certain physical characteristics. In short, she did not feel deeply interested in her. Nonetheless, she garnered her helping energies to focus on her concerns and deliberately and thoughtfully attended to the helpee, both nonverbally and verbally, by sitting forward in her chair, leaning forward toward the helpee, and maintaining eye contact. Her facial expression was concerned, and her voice was warm. She felt the helpee was a person in need, and each person in need deserves attention, close listening, and respect. Remember the message to be conveyed is a simple one: "I am interested in you."

Conveying "With-ness"

Beyond listening, nonverbal attending behavior can convey a sense of "with-ness," or rapport, between helper and helpee. Nonverbal communication has aptly been called a *relationship language* (Ekman & Friesen, 1969). This means that one can discover where one is "at" with someone else by observing nonverbal communication. Two individuals conversing with little body movement, standing five feet from each other, both looking around, are probably not involved in a close interpersonal transaction. At that moment, there is little rapport between the people. Another pair of people—one nodding to the other, smiling as the other smiles, moving forward as the other gets closer—is more likely to be engaged in a mutually involving interaction. Rapport exists at this point in their relationship.

The second example is closer to the helping relationship. Nonverbal reciprocity is characteristic of nonverbal behavior in a helping context. The helper generally attempts to match his or her nonverbal behavior to that of the helpee. By matching, we mean that the helper's nonverbal response will be congruent with the helpee's message. If the helpee is upset, the helper will demonstrate supportive concern by looking serious, by speaking softly, by gently touching the helpee. If the helpee has just had an exciting experience, the helper will smile and convey enthusiasm by an animated voice tone. The helper thus shows he or she is "with" the helpee.

Imagine yourself with a helper. Let's say you have just heard that your father is very ill. You mention this to the helper, who booms loudly "That's too bad." You are taken aback by the tone. Your feeling is "He's not with me; I wonder if he heard me right." When voice tone is inconsistent with helpee feelings, the helpee becomes confused. On the other hand, imagine yourself with a different helper who says in a quiet, tender tone, "That's too bad." You likely feel that he is in tune with you, and that he has not only heard what you said but has also sensed your upset. Consequently, you feel a rapport with the helper. Conveying "with-ness" is essential to the facilitation of an effective helping relationship.

Encouraging Exploration and Discussion

Nonverbal behavior is also facilitative in helping by encouraging the helpee to continue talking. A person would not want to explore personal concerns with someone who seems disinterested. This aspect of nonverbal behavior presents the helpee with feedback as to whether the helper is concerned with learning more. The helper can influence the helpee's disclosure by signaling interest or disinterest in further exploration.

Perhaps the most common nonverbal cue for encouragement is the head nod. Consider how often the listener nods in an animated conversation. The speaker or discloser will occasionally pause and look to the other person for a cue: "Can I keep going? Am I boring you? Do you have something to add? Do you agree?" With a simple head nod, these questions are answered and the conversation continues. But nonverbal cues are quick to reveal the truth: even if the helper is nodding at appropriate moments, a helpee will pause if the helper glances at a watch.

The helper, then, reinforces by nonverbal behavior the verbal behavior of the helpee. The message is "Continue. I'm interested in hearing more." The basic ground rule of the relationship has been silently formulated in this way. Nonverbal behavior is used to communicate a general message of sincere interest and to encourage a deeper exploration of the helpee's concerns.

Differential Reinforcing

During the initial phase of helping, the helper is interested in finding out as much about the helpee as possible. The helper may rightly believe that early conclusions about the helpee's problems will be premature and inadequate. Problems are never simple, and many helpees are confused about what really concerns them, so the helper is employing the correct initial strategy by being "nondirective." In other words, the helper encourages the helpee to talk at great length about pressing concerns. Nonverbal attending allows this to happen.

As mentioned previously, the helper is most interested in hearing as much as possible from the helpee early in a helping relationship, particularly in the Entry (Stage 1) and Exploration (Stage 2) Stages. By leaning forward, nodding the head as a cue to continue, maintaining eye contact, keeping responses brief, and so on, the helper promotes the talking of the helpee. During these stages the helper generally does not direct the focus or content of the helpee's talk, for doing so might cause the loss of valuable information about the helpee. What does the helpee bring up spontaneously? What does the helpee present as the pressing concerns or goals? What issues does the helpee fail to raise? The helper's nonverbal attending behavior reinforces the helpee for talking about and sharing feelings and ideas.

Remembering that nonverbal attending is an encouragement to further discussion, the helper may wish to employ nonverbal behavior differently at a later point in a helping relationship. If attending can encourage talking, so can it discourage.

For example, in the Clarification Stage (Stage 3) the helper may find the helpee rambling and failing to focus on any one issue. Rather than offering positive reinforcement to the helpee for any and all talk, the helper may selectively attend to only that talk which is salient to the issue currently at hand. Similarly, after the helpee and helper have decided in the Integration Stage (Stage 4) on goals, the helper may use nonverbal attending to selectively reinforce various plans in the Program Planning Stage (Stage 5). Maintaining eye contact and leaning forward when the helpee makes a relevant statement will reinforce the helpee for focusing on that issue or concern. Inattentive behaviors like leaning back, dropping eye contact, not nodding one's head will convey the message that the helper is not interested in following up that particular topic. In later chapters, it will be clear that certain verbal responses can add additional impact and clarity to these messages. For the moment, it is important to recognize the power and use of nonverbal behaviors.

What we are suggesting is that a helper can employ nonverbal attending as a *differential reinforcer*. That is, the helper can respond enthusiastically nonverbally in order to positively reinforce certain helpee ideas and behaviors and can reply less enthusiastically or even ignore other ideas and behaviors.

Another example: an employment counselor wishes to encourage a client to go to several job interviews. The client is ambivalent. In talking, the helper nods affirmatively and smiles as the client discusses the possible advantages of going to be interviewed. When the problems involved in going on interviews come up, the counselor responds politely but in an unenthusiastic way. The helper gives no smiles and speaks in a bit of a monotone. The client talks briefly about anticipated problems but returns to the advantages. He decides to go ahead with the interviews. The counselor *could* have responded with much interest in the problems, but it would not have been helpful. Instead, the helper's lack of nonverbal attention served to discourage the helpee from following this avenue of thought. Nonverbal behaviors were used to differentially reinforce positive vs. negative approaches to planning and taking action.

HOW DO VERBAL AND NONVERBAL BEHAVIORS RELATE?

In conveying listening and "with-ness" as well as in encouraging exploration and differential reinforcement of thoughts, nonverbal cues are enmeshed to varying degrees with verbal ones. They are always intertwined in helping. Specific ways in which nonverbal cues relate to words illustrate how the communication messages discussed above are transmitted to the helpee. The following are several ways in which verbal and nonverbal behaviors are related (based on information in Knapp, 1972).

Repeating

The helper says to the helpee "I feel close to you at this moment" and then *moves physically closer* to the helpee. The helper's nonverbal behaviors *repeat* the verbal behaviors. The nonverbal message is then a strengthening of the verbal message. No new message is added; rather, the original message is reiterated in a different manner.

Contradicting

A helper professes interest in the helpee's concern by saying, for example, "Let me hear all about it" and then accepts a phone call. The helper has nonverbally *contradicted* the stated intent of the verbal message. The same is true of helpers who verbally open the door and then avoid eye contact, sneak glances at watches or appointment books, doodle on notepaper, and so on; their nonverbal behavior belies their verbal messages. People are highly sensitive to such contradictions, which are called the *"leakage" of actual thoughts and feelings* (Ekman & Friesen, 1969). Helpees are usually very sensitive to this, especially since they already feel vulnerable by having revealed personal concerns to someone whose role it is to be interested. Consider the converse of the example given above regarding repeating. If a helper says "I feel close to you at this moment" and then leans backwards and away in the chair, what message is likely to be received?

Substituting

When a helper nods, this nonverbal behavior *substitutes* for the words "Go on. I am listening." An honestly felt smile from the helper is an excellent way of communicating "I'm happy for you." In general, nonverbal behavior is an important *substitute channel for communicating emotion*—especially intense emotions difficult to put into words. How do you generally express elation, excitement, surprise? Bereavement, grief, displeasure? Think about the nonverbal gestures you make when you immediately experience these feelings. Helpers sometimes substitute such nonverbal expressions for simpler emotions and occasionally for more intense ones.

Complementing

A helper praises a helpee and then gently hugs the person. This nonverbal expression *adds to the helper's words*, letting the helpee know that the helper means what was said. It is not repeating, for the hug does not reiterate the message of praise. Rather, it *complements* the praise, conveying the message "I feel good with you and about you." Complementing verbal behaviors through nonverbal ones provides additional messages about the helping relationship.

Accenting

Certain parts of verbal communication can be given *special emphasis* or accent by the helper. *Accenting* serves to communicate the particular importance of the verbal message. Voice tone is a particularly effective nonverbal accenting tool. For example, "I'd suggest you think that through again" can be said in a harsh, loud, threatening way; the message implied is that the helpee has no choice. Or, it can be said in a quiet, bland, uninterested way; the message implied is that the helper is not particularly concerned. Hand movements are accenting behaviors, underlining verbal points. All of us have had some experience with the "finger pointer" who pokes a finger at us while telling us what we should or shouldn't be doing. The effective helper will avoid this kind of accenting, but may emphasize certain ideas with other hand gestures. For instance, a drug counselor may be talking with a long-term helpee who has just threatened to begin using heroin again. While saying "In no way would I like to see you start again—I'd be sorely disappointed," the counselor slices the air horizontally with his hand. Such a gesture accents the verbal message. Facial expressions can serve this purpose as well.

Relating and Regulating

Partial control of an ongoing verbal discussion can be accomplished by the use of nonverbal behavior. A head nod, as mentioned above, is an excellent regulator, suggesting to the helpee to continue talking. A shrug of the shoulders may encourage the helpee to pause and then think through an idea more carefully. This is the *feedback function* of nonverbal communication. It provides regulatory information to both helper and helpee about their ongoing conversation: "Do I go on?" "Do I stop now?" "Is it your turn to share your thoughts?" Nonverbal gestures can *relate* such information in a swift fashion, without verbal disruption.

In Sum

Nonverbal behavior, then, can communicate several general messages to the helpee about how the helper feels and thinks. The helpee will leave an initial meeting sensing whether or not the helper feels interested in him or her; whether or not the helper appears confident, competent, and concerned; and whether or not the helper is a trustworthy person. Nonverbal cues are a major part of the overall first impression, one which will affect the remainder of the helping relationship. Nonverbal behaviors will continue to repeat and accent these messages, as well as convey new ones as the helping relationship proceeds. Given the vital importance of nonverbal behavior, it is imperative that helpers be able to use it effectively.

WHAT IS EFFECTIVE NONVERBAL BEHAVIOR?

Using nonverbal behavior effectively entails striking a balance between how the helper might naturally act nonverbally and which nonverbal behaviors might be most facilitative for the helpee in the helping relationship. The helper's comfort is very important, since it's hard to be an effective helper if one is anxious; the more natural one acts, the less anxious one is likely to become. However, the helper's comfort is really secondary to conveying to the helpee a sense of undistracted, sincere concern.

Many examples occur of automatic but usually comfortable behavior that are ineffective or truly destructive, such as folding one's arms across one's chest. Another frequent automatic behavior is wrapping one's legs around those of the chair. One striking example was that of a student who insisted on crossing his legs at the knee with one leg angled up toward his face, the ankle resting on the opposite knee. Simultaneously, his arms were looped under his knee and ankle. He sometimes rested his chin on the upper knee. If this stance sounds contorted and uncomfortable, it certainly appeared that way to the authors and to his classmates who observed that they felt distanced from him when he talked. His physical position put them off. As a matter of fact, most felt that they were looked down on and not listened to. This surprised the student, for he believed this position to convey a message of casual naturalness and "with-ness." Unfortunately, most of his classmates felt he was distracted from their concerns, if not hiding from them; that is, they felt his posture created barriers between them. His nonverbal attending behaviors were highly ineffective. Yet ineffective nonverbal behaviors *can* be changed. The first step is to become aware of facilitative nonverbal helping behaviors. Following this, the helper can decide on and work toward any necessary changes.

There are several aspects of our nonverbal selves that have communicational importance in helping. Personal nonverbal communication cues in helping lie in situational cues and interactive cues. These are:

Situational cues:
1. physical appearance
2. clothing we choose to wear

Interactive cues:
3. eyes and how we use them
4. touch and what we allow ourselves to do
5. body movement
6. vocal quality

Physical appearance and clothing are sets of nonverbal cues that are "given" by the time the helping interaction begins. The helper should give some thought to appropriate clothing before meeting a helpee, but after that these nonverbal cues change little. These cues are called *situational* in that they present the helpee with a predetermined situation. The remaining nonverbal behaviors can be termed *interactive* in that they occur during the actual helping interaction. These cues are those over which the helper has the most direct continuing control. They are also the most critical to an effective helping interaction.

We also employ aspects of our environment to communicate to others. Certain *environmental cues* are particularly important and may even be seen as having interactive significance. These are:

Environmental cues:
7. distance
8. time

These diverse cues are used as nonverbal media for communicating. We will discuss effective nonverbal helping behavior for each of these personal and environmental sets of cues.

SITUATIONAL CUES

Physical Appearance

A helper's physical attributes are undeniably important to initial helping relationships. Age, sex, race, size, and attractiveness are among the physical stimuli that the helpee reacts to. These cues immediately tell the helpee something about the helper. Exactly what they say depends on the particular helpee. Each helpee has certain cues that mean more than others, resulting from past history and experience as well as beliefs. This nonverbal aspect of the person is a communication message over which the helper has little control.

Some examples of the messages *received*, but *not intended to be sent*, are:

Helper Physical Appearance Cue		Possible Negative Message Received by Helpee
Age	older	"How can someone this old understand me?"
	younger	"Does this person know enough about life to help me?"
Sex	male	"I've just had a fight with my husband. How could I be open with another male?"
	female	"Would a woman really be able to help me? I wonder what her husband is like."
Race	White	"This guy has never set one foot in a ghetto. He's probably out to screw me."
	Black	"This counselor is Black. What gives him the right to tell a White person what to do?"
Overall Appearance	attractive	"This guy's a real turn-on. I'd sure like to have him worrying about me."
	unattractive	"I really feel sorry for *him*. He must be a lonely person."

These interpretations on the basis of physical cues emphasize the possibility of the helpee perceiving the helper in a way that may interfere with the relationship.

Yet interference need not be the case. Such cues may also allow the helpee to feel more comfortable, to have less concern about the helper's competence, and to facilitate the formation of a helping relationship.

Let's look at these same cues, hypothesizing the possibility of positive influences.

Helper Physical Appearance Cue		*Possible Positive Message Received by Helpee*
Age	older	"This person is old enough to have a lot of wisdom. I bet she can be really helpful."
	younger	"This helper is close to my age and will really be able to understand."
Sex	male	"I always feel more at ease with a man. I'm glad it isn't a woman."
	female	"I always feel more at ease with a woman. I'm glad it isn't a man."
Race	White	"Even though we're different races, I bet this person can help me understand the White world in addition to better understanding myself."
	Black	"Some of the troubles I've had have been racial. Maybe I'll learn something from this person that'll help me in my work."
Overall Appearance	attractive	"It's pleasant to be with someone attractive, but it's funny how unimportant it is to me."
	unattractive	"This person isn't particularly good-looking, but it doesn't matter to me."

Whichever message is received depends on the helpee. Think about your own reactions to these cues. What messages do you receive?

The effects of physical appearance *per se* are probably transient—they primarily affect first impressions. Most helpees are more concerned with the specific helpfulness of the helper than with physical attributes, although, of course, some helpees allow their first impressions to unduly control them. While helpees with strong initial reactions to physical characteristics will often revise their impression later, it is important to recognize these reactions. Helpers must understand what their physical appearance communicates. Effective helpers will be alert to helpee cues indicating the interference of messages based on physical attributes. Such interference needs to be brought into the open and dealt with. Hopefully, it will no longer be a problem. Other nonverbal cues play a far larger role in the ongoing quality of the relationship than do physical attributes. This occurs in part because the helpee recognizes that the helper's physical appearance cannot be changed whereas other nonverbal behaviors seem under the helper's control.

Clothing

Clothing is often viewed as reflecting one's personality, attitudes, or values. Clothing may be used for decoration, protection, sexual attraction, self-assertion, group identification, or display of status or role (Knapp, 1972). In terms of a helpee's reaction, however, several of these uses may have an important impact, regardless of whether such use is a conscious one. In particular, group identification and display of status or role may well affect an initial helping interaction. Let's look at these two aspects of clothing separately.

1. *Clothing as an indicator of social group.* Our clothing tells others the type of *social group* we belong to. Even though we may not actually choose our clothes to reflect this, people do tend to dress in accord with their reference group norms. A helper's attire will convey to the helpee a certain set of preconceptions, attitudes, and values about this particular helper, even though these thoughts and feelings may not be accurate. Take a helper wearing bluejeans as an example. Jeans are informal attire. A helper who feels comfortable enough to wear jeans may have certain advantages working with high school or college students that a helper in a three-piece suit would immediately forfeit. Students would probably perceive the first helper as belonging to a social group more similar to their own. Talking to this type of helper might be facilitated because of the social meaning of clothing. However, their perceptions of the suited helper would probably focus on differences in social group, so talking might be inhibited. Types of clothes are not clear visual cues but rather are inferable clues regarding social group.

2. *Clothing as an indicator of status.* A good example of the use of clothing as a *status cue* can be seen by the use of uniforms by those in some helping professions. In addition to its group-identification value, a uniform presents a helpee with a very clear visual cue that says "I'm different from you." The message implies: "Respond to this helper as one would to someone in a specific role." The uniform serves a clarifying function, then, suggesting to the helpee what to expect and how to act. It may increase the value of a particular helper where perceived expertise is important to the helpee. Role—that of "expert" in a particular field—is clearly "labeled" by the uniform.

Uniforms, however, simultaneously decrease the value of a helper *as a person,* so the personal aspect of the helping relationship may suffer. The most prevalent initial result of a uniform is one of distancing the helpee from the helper. In some situations, this may be intended. The necessity for uniforms is probably clearest when there is some value in making the helper's role salient. For example, it makes sense for a police officer to wear a uniform since it should be obvious to a lawbreaker that this person represents the law. However, in helping situations where interpersonal interaction is stressed, a uniform will add little to the helper's effectiveness.

Control Over Clothing. Some professionals are allowed little control over clothes—for example, nurses. Even in nursing, though, restrictions are slowly being lifted. Yet some helpers in nursing still find it difficult to express their personal identity given the remaining prevalent norms. One nurse we know bought several brightly colored uniforms, feeling more comfortable in these than in regulation white. However, her experiences with other nurses when she wore these uniforms were so unpleasant that she felt less and less at ease with them and began to wear her white uniforms more often again. Thus, while she attempted to control her clothing, believing the colored uniforms might have a less distancing impact on her patients than the white ones, she found it difficult to maintain control within her professional reference group.

Yet clothes are a set of nonverbal cues over which most helpers do have control. We can choose to dress more or less formally, more or less colorfully, more or less stylishly, and so on. We can choose our clothes to express something of our inner beings or to play down our personal selves. We can choose our clothes to suggest belonging to particular social groups or to a particular social status.

However, clothing's critical role in helping is easily overstated. As with physical appearance, the effective helper will be alert to how his or her style of dress is perceived. Research on clothing suggests that stereotypical responses to differing clothing types occur, especially with strangers, while clothing is of secondary importance for the maintenance of relationships with acquaintances and friends. Clothing aids in initially setting the stage and is very important in the earliest contact between helper and helpee. Other "person-related" cues, called *interactive cues,* are more relevant later on than are physical appearance and clothing.

INTERACTIVE CUES

Eyes

Probably the most important use of the eyes in a helping communication is *eye contact.* Eyes are vitally important, first, because of their general expressiveness and, second, because they are a primary source of nonverbal "leakage." They say a lot, often more than the content of our words. We look to other people's eyes for clues of their intent. Our associations between eye contact behaviors and meaning are strong: looking away connotes shame or embarrassment, looking down connotes sadness, looking directly at someone suggests honesty, staring may reveal hostility. The helper looks to the helpee's eyes for nonverbal clues about feelings, and the helpee looks to the helper's eyes for nonverbal messages, usually of confirmation or contradiction of the words the helper speaks.

In helping, eye contact serves several functions (based on information in Knapp, 1972).

1. *Feedback.* After talking, the helpee will often pause, make eye contact, and wait for feedback of some kind about what was said. Does the helper seem to be listening? Is the helper interested? By making contact, the helpee will immediately discover whether or not the helper was listening. If the helpee finds the helper looking concerned, often with slightly furrowed brows, the helpee will continue. If the helpee's attempt to obtain feedback finds the helper looking elsewhere, there will be less incentive for the helpee to continue. In order to demonstrate listening and convey "with-ness," it is vital that the helper maintain eye contact.

Another kind of feedback is more qualitative. The helper's eye contact may reveal judgment of what the helpee says. For example, if the helper looks down, the helpee may believe the helper to be embarrassed and would likely stop speaking on that particular topic. In fact, the helper may *not* be embarrassed, but the helpee's perceptions and interpretations of this nonverbal signal will strongly affect the direction of the interaction. Optimally, the helper gives initial feedback about being interested and concerned to encourage the helpee to continue talking. Judgments about the helpee must be avoided.

2. *Conversation flow.* Eye contact can tell the helpee if the helper wants to talk or prefers that the helpee continue. With very subtle cues, we can communicate our interest to influence a conversation. A helper's turning away of eye contact following fairly steady contact will be a powerful message to a helpee indicating that the helper wishes to stop talking. Effective helpers tend to use eye contact steadily while both talking and listening.

3. *Clues about the relationship.* Eye contact provides clues about the nature of the relationship between people, particularly the closeness between helper and helpee. The helper may be telling the helpee about his or her interest or involvement with the helpee, depending on the kind and quality of helper eye contact. Since we tend to look at people we like more than those we don't, the helpee will associate eye contact with liking. Eye contact can be one important message to the helpee that a personal—that is, close—relationship is desired by the helper.

In a sense, eye contact places a demand upon the helpee to reciprocate. That is, the helpee is nonverbally invited to become involved in the relationship. Because of this, some helpees become anxious if too much eye contact is given and some become anxious with any eye contact at all, thinking it demands a level of closeness that the helpee may be unable to offer. Early on, in one helping relationship, it became quite clear that the helpee was frightened of close contact. From the very beginning he averted his eyes and kept them averted. Yet he was open in the initial session about his embarrassment in being in a psychologist's office discussing very personal feelings. The helper, while understanding, felt frustrated in trying to reach this man in a personal way via eye contact. Even in demonstrating understanding, one avenue of cues from helper to helpee was cut off. The helper can nonetheless offer the invitation and, if rebuffed (intentionally or not) by the helpee, the helper still has important information about the helpee and can thereby modify the approach.

Further information about this same helpee's feelings came about through his continued lack of eye contact. Looking directly at the helper was too anxiety-producing for the helpee, so he continued to avert his eyes. During a discussion about relationships, the helper broached the subject of eye contact and its role in the development of close relationships. The helpee was aware of his nonverbal communication but felt inadequate to change it at that time. The helper continued to focus her eyes naturally on the helpee's face and eyes when the helpee spoke and when she herself spoke: the invitation was maintained.

Effective Eye Contact. Effective eye contact means that the eyes of the helper focus on the helpee in a sincere, relaxed way. *When the helpee is talking, the helper looks right at him or her.* However, the helper does not stare or remain fixed in eye contact. Such a set of cues might lead the helpee to feel like an object. Indeed, most of us get uneasy if someone *never* breaks eye contact. Eye contact, then, should essentially be relaxed though deliberate. Effective eye contact facilitates interaction; little eye contact or too steady eye contact inhibits it. Helpers must attend to the helpee's nonverbal response to their eye contact. If the helpee appears threatened by the type or amount of eye contact, it should be modified.

Research on the role that eyes play in communication suggests that we maintain eye contact when listening and tend to look away at times when speaking. We look away to think, to clear our visual field from cues that may interfere with our thoughts. However, in a helping situation, *maintaining eye contact in responding* as a helper is essential. In fact, it is a powerful interpersonal act because it promotes the helpee to remain attentive to the helper. People's eyes are drawn to one another's eyes. Maintaining eye contact when speaking maintains the continuity of the interaction and may well increase the intimacy of the discussion. This is one specific area of visual behavior in which many helpers can and must increase their nonverbal effectiveness.

Touch

The role of touch in helping is rather complex, resulting from the associations to touch we have in our culture. Our norms for touching are rather strict, especially for strangers or casual acquaintances. Since we associate touching with closeness and affection, most of us reserve touch for personally close or intimate relationships. Because touch can convey meanings ranging from encouragement through liking to loving, however, it can add richness to a helping relationship.

Touching is the most personal of the nonverbal behaviors the helper can use. It is a behavior that the helpee will be *sharply* aware of, unlike physical proximity or eye contact. It is also a behavior that the helpee will directly associate to the helper's feelings about him or her. In other words, the helpee sees the helper reaching out in a personal, direct way. In our culture, only people who are close to others do this. Therefore, the helpee may think "This person must feel close to me." Touching can be a facilitator of closeness, an invitation to the helpee to engage in a meaningful relationship, and a declaration of the helper's personal caring.

In one helping relationship, touch played an essential role in conveying personal caring. The helpee involved was engaged in examining her most intimate relationships and working through her ambivalence about them. In doing so, she needed reassurance from time to time that she was still lovable and could still elicit caring in a close relationship. A gentle but firm touch on her shoulder, a pat on her hand, and an occasional hug around her shoulders were important to her: these nonverbal cues told her that she was indeed cared about and could maintain closeness in a relationship. She said that they helped her through the crisis of analysis and change in her relationships outside of the helping relationship.

Another helpee asked for such contact. This helpee was also concerned with his most intimate relationships but was having an even more difficult time confronting his role in maintaining painful patterns of interaction. At times his need for human contact as well as reassurance was so powerful that he requested a hug before continuing to explore his behaviors and avenues of change.

Touch played yet a different role with a third helpee. This helpee was learning progressive muscular relaxation techniques. In order to assess his level of relaxation, in addition to his subjective ratings and description, the helper evaluated his physical relaxation through touch. For example, she lifted his hands and arms and let them fall to their original position to assess looseness. She felt his shoulders to assess flexibility, and so on. This contact had little to do with the content of the helpee's concerns, but was directly related to one agreed-upon goal in the helping relationship: learning deep muscle relaxation in order to decrease tension. The helper's willingness to initiate such contact, however, no doubt conveyed a personal message as well: "I am relaxed with you."

Some helpees may not receive the message as it is intended. The variability in our response to and use of touch is considerable. Some helpees may become uneasy if the helper expresses feelings through touching. One of the authors, for example, experienced difficulty around this issue with a helpee who was quite fearful of intimacy. There had been several occasions when the helper felt a spontaneous urge to touch him, times when the helpee was expressing very distressing and painful feelings and was clearly feeling isolated. However, the helper held back from actually making contact because the helpee's nonverbal message throughout had been a strong "Keep away." At one point, however, the helpee himself raised the issue of fearing touch. The helper explored it with him and in so doing reached out and touched his knee. The helpee's reaction was calm; because it had gone at his own pace, he was comfortable with it. The helper made appropriate use of touch without threatening the helping relationship.

Helpers must be perceptive of their helpees' responses to touching and must moderate it carefully. A helper at ease with physical contact may need to limit touching with certain helpees. A helper afraid of such contact might work on increasing tactile communication behaviors. When used appropriately, touching can create a close bond between helper and helpee.

Body Movement

As with other nonverbal behaviors, the communicative value of body movement, or *kinesics,* is a function of cultural and personal norms. In helping situations, body movement can be an important means of expressing the helper's accessibility, degree of relaxation, and concern for closeness with the helpee. Kinesic cues may also be clues to the helper's unexpressed and hidden intent.

Open arms are associated with accessibility to communication, at least for seated people. A helper with arms across the chest presents a visual stimulus that may be giving an unintended message of defensiveness or of being closed off. A forward lean is a similar sign of helper accessibility. If the helper leans far backward in a chair, lack of interest may be communicated. By leaning toward the helpee, the helper is demonstrating an interest in really "hearing" what the helpee says.

It is easier for the helpee to feel liked if the helper uses posture to encourage the perception of being heard, interested in, and having an accessible helper. While a helper's arms should most often be uncrossed, lean position can vary more. While leaning back past an upright position should be avoided, several degrees of forward lean are possible. Leaning a bit forward from the vertical is the most effective general reinforcer for maintaining the helpee's involvement. An extreme forward lean is best used as a specific encourager to continue talking and to perceive the helper as very involved. Sideways leans might best be avoided, since they may connote a status difference because people often use them with lower status persons.

Degrees of tension are also shown by body movement. Rigidity of posture can communicate an unintended attitude of dislike to the helpee. On the other hand, sloppiness of posture or excessive relaxation may present the helpee with a different impression. In this case, the helper may appear *too* casual, *too* relaxed. The helpee may feel that a person in a helping role should be somewhat more alert and attentive.

Essential to the communication of concern are head nods and smiles. Both of these kinesic behaviors are associated with a person's affiliative efforts—that is, his or her interest in getting to know another person. In addition, a helper conveys considerable interpersonal warmth with a smile. Both behaviors, of course, must be used relatively sparingly. Excessive head nodding may prove annoying to the helpee, perhaps giving the opposite message: that the helper has heard enough. Too much smiling may say that the helpee's concerns are taken too lightly. When used appropriately, however, these cues can have a major impact on the helpee's view of the helper's concerns.

Appropriate use of head nods or smiles includes keeping them to a minimum (especially head nods). Beginning helpers often overuse head nods, bobbing their heads at every statement or even every phrase. Feedback from their helpees usually makes it clear that such incessant head nodding is distracting. In addition, many of the helpees noted that they began to feel unlistened to; they began to perceive the head nodding as paying lip service to the idea of listening while the helper was really thinking about other things. Examining helper intent revealed a deep and genuine interest, which was unfortunately not effectively conveyed.

The same is true with smiles. Novice helpers too frequently smile either at irrelevant times or whenever they would smile in a conversation with a friend. The guideline to remember is that helping interactions have different goals than do friendship interactions. Certainly, helpers may smile when they are feeling warm toward their helpees, or they are amused by anecdotes their helpees are relating, or they are matching the helpee's mood. Sometimes, however, the helping goals contradict these common sense norms. For instance, if a helpee tends to avoid serious exploration by telling funny stories, the helper may want to decrease such behavior by not smiling at the anecdote and maintaining a more serious expression. This is an example of differential reinforcement. Of course, the helper should make an observation regarding the helpee's avoidance behavior so the two of them could explore it. Feedback to the helper would include decreased use of anecdotes and smiles by the helpee.

In a converse situation, one helping goal may be to promote a less serious, more relaxed view of oneself and the world in a helpee who maintains constant ill-humor or no humor about himself/herself. By using smiles at opportune moments, the helper may facilitate some change in the helpee. Feedback to the helper in this relationship would include observations of greater frequency of smiling and mildly increasing use of humor by the helpee.

Appropriate usage of nods and smiles is, then, difficult to pinpoint. Excessive use is fairly easy to observe while less than optimal use is more difficult to observe. Too somber an expression, no use of humor, and stiffness in body movement are some indicators. Awareness of helpee responses will augment feedback to the helper and assist in monitoring such kinesic behaviors.

Finally, body movement is a source of information about the helper's real intent and feelings. Legs and feet have been found to be good signs of "leakage" because we are not accustomed to monitoring their action. For instance, shifting one's feet several times may signal boredom to a perceptive helpee. Crossing one's leg in the opposite direction to the helpee's sometimes suggests distance or opposition.

We are reminded of the initial helping session with a couple, both of whom had been seen for some time individually by each of the two helpers involved in the session. Observing various nonverbal cues regarding degree of tension in the new situation, one helper noted that the legs of each person were crossed at the knee in a very particular pattern. The wife and her psychotherapist crossed their legs toward one another, while the husband and his counselor crossed their legs toward each other. Simultaneously, the direction of leg crossing was away from that of the other two. Whenever one of the helpers switched directions, so did both the helpees. The simplest message of this pattern of body movement among the foursome was that each helper-helpee pair that had already been working together was more comfortable with one another than with the members of the other pair. On a different level, a possible message communicated by the pattern was that there was distance and tension between the wife and husband, each of whom chose to ally with a helper rather than with each other. The helpers commented on the observed pattern of behavior, and an open discussion of the felt distance and hostility between spouses ensued.

As with all the nonverbal behaviors, the helper needs to be keenly aware of his or her own specific body language and how it seems to be affecting the helpee—or how it *may* affect the helpee. In general, the effective use of body movement entails the spontaneous and expressive use of the body. Extraneous behaviors (for example, excessive hand gestures), distracting behaviors (for example, fidgeting), behaviors implying disinterest (for example, leaning away), and behaviors distancing helper from helpee (for example, crossing one's arms) need to be avoided. Forward leaning, posture directly facing the helpee, open arm placement, spontaneous smiles, and appropriate head nods are examples of kinesic behaviors worth employing in helping.

Vocal Quality

The vocal quality of our words is critical to their meaning. One cannot always know what people *really* mean unless their manner of saying it is taken into account. In a helping situation, more so than in ordinary conversation, *consistency* between what a helper *says* and what is *meant* needs to be high. The effective helper does not communicate in a contradictory fashion. Therefore, particular attention must be given to the tone of voice employed in speaking to be sure that it complements the verbal message. If the person says "I'm really happy for you" in a dispassionate way, the helpee will not only disbelieve the message but will also question the helper's honesty. Saying "I'm really happy for you" in an enthused, sparkling tone is consistent and complementary. The helpee is more likely to believe the message and to sense helper sincerity.

General vocal tone can be looked at in another way. Vocal cues can communicate whether or not the helper is truly understanding the helpee. This can be accomplished if the helper matches his or her verbal tone to the helpee's. For example, a depressed helpee, talking slowly and cheerlessly, would resent a helper's cheerful, animated response. Alternately, a helpee who had just had a successful experience might be inhibited by a helper who came across in a deeply serious, formal way. Helpers talking too fast may confuse their helpees; helpers talking too slowly may bore them. Vocal tone, then, can be an index of the seriousness of the interaction, and the helper should generally agree to the helpee's definition of the seriousness of the interaction in early interviews, especially in the Entry Stage (Stage 1). As the helping relationship progresses, the helper may sometimes find a need to challenge or confront the helpee in this definition. Differential use of vocal tone will be one tool in so doing.

A final area in which vocal quality is important is in speech disturbances, an aspect of the nonverbal side of speech. Some examples are given below (based on information in Mahl, 1959):

Disturbance	Example
1. *"Ah"* (also "eh," "uh," "uhm")	"As I was saying . . . ah . . . ."
2. *Sentence change*	"You're feeling . . . . What's his name?"
3. *Repetition*	"You're like your . . . like your father."
4. *Stutter*	"I . . . I . . . I don't know."
5. *Omission* (parts of words left out)	"She was embar . . . . I thought she was embarrassed."
6. *Sentence incompletion* (an expression is interrupted, clearly left incomplete)	"I saw him when he . . . Then we talked for a while."
7. *Tongue slips* (includes neologisms, transposition of entire words from correct place in sentence, substitution of an unintended word)	"I was lying" (said instead of "I was trying").
8. *Intruding incoherent* sound	"You've been experiencing (ach) much excitement lately."

Since we perceive many of these behaviors as reflecting anxiety, helpers emitting them may be seen as being uncomfortable and unsure of themselves and therefore need to monitor their own speech. Checking the frequency of such responses and working toward decreasing them are hallmarks of effective helpers.

Vocal cues must be deliberately employed to facilitate the communicative channels of the interview. Poor vocal cues may confuse or annoy the helpee, to the detriment of the relationship. They can communicate a message that contradicts the helper's words and can raise questions about the helper's sincerity. Effective use of vocal cues can serve to facilitate understanding, to clarify helper meaning, and to underline the verbal messages the helper sends. They can also promote closeness between helper and helpee.

ENVIRONMENTAL CUES

Distance

Careful use of interpersonal distance between helper and helpee can facilitate the helping interaction. In general, we sit closer to people with whom we feel comfortable, whom we like, and in whom we are interested. Furthermore, distance is associated with status; that is, people of different status will stand or sit farther apart than will peers. By sitting close to the helpee, the helper is utilizing these implicit norms. The helper is behaving as a concerned, interested peer would, increasing psychological closeness by decreasing physical distance.

If the helper sits too far away, say 10 feet, the formality of the interaction is emphasized. The message is "I don't want to get too close. Let's keep it impersonal." On the other hand, if the helper sits too close, perhaps 1½ feet away, the message may also be counterproductive: "I want to control you" is one possible message received by the helpee. Such close distances tend to make most people step back quickly since their "personal space" or "territory" has been invaded (Sommer, 1969). Most of us feel such an invasion permissible only with certain people, those we like and choose to have "close." In helping, such a distance might be quite threatening and embarrassing since it may connote excessive interpersonal intimacy. Therefore, increases in physical closeness will encourage interpersonal closeness up to a certain point at which the helpee defines the distance as that reserved for personally intimate relationships. The helper can encourage closeness by proximity but must attend to cues from the helpee about this comfortable personal distance. Cues may include the helpee shifting backwards in the chair or couch, leaning away, looking away, and so on. Sometimes a helpee may actually get up and move. If the distance is too great, opposite cues may be observed: for example, helpee leaning forward toward the helper. Again, the helper needs to be alert to these cues and moderate her or his behavior accordingly.

Time

In addition to distance, time is an environmental cue which can convey important interpersonal messages. *Status* is often communicated by time. For example, an executive might not be too concerned over being late for an appointment with a secretary, although the secretary might even be early. Making a helpee wait may lead to several reactions —some helpful, others less so. The helpee may "read" the message as evidence of the helper's importance or expertise. On the other hand, the helpee may begin to question the helper's caring. A helpee who wonders about a helper's interest is in a difficult position. For example, a helper may ask a helpee to discuss current feelings when the most prominent feelings regard resentment about being made to wait. The relationship would then begin with a strain. Any status attributed to the helper in this way might well be outweighed by the negative consequences.

Use of time *within* interactions can have an important effect on outcome. Interviews are generally of a finite time nature and the time is, in a sense, divided between the two participants. *Control* of the interview is conveyed by the use of time. The helper can control the way in which the time of the interview is spent. The more the helper speaks, the less the helpee can speak. If the helper uses more time, the message given the helpee may be "This is for my benefit. I want to know certain things and I want to tell you certain things." In some cases, this may be appropriate; however, for most interviews the opposite message would be more important. This is especially true in the first four stages (Entry, Exploration, Clarification, and Interpretation). It remains almost as true in the latter four (Program Planning, Action-Taking, Review, and Termination), although in these stages the helper takes somewhat more of a leading role than that previously taken.

To convey the message that the interview is for the benefit of the helpee, helpers must be aware of the length of their remarks. Short, succinct responses can elicit much information *and* simultaneously convey to the helpee the helper's willingness to listen. To be sure, lengthy remarks, detailed questions, or speeches by the helper give a very different sense of who's in charge of the discussion.

Another major effect that time can have on an interview is in terms of *pacing*. Probably the best example is in terms of the role silences play in helping interactions. Most people fill conversational silences quickly; after the passage of a certain amount of time, discomfort arises unless someone says something. In a helping interaction, such conversational etiquette may be unhelpful. Most often, a silence will be followed by a further response by the helpee if the helper does not respond immediately. When silences occur, the pacing of the interaction is being formulated. Many helpers, uncomfortable with such pauses, rush in to move the discussion along. However, the helper who waits without filling the silence implicitly places the responsibility upon the helpee. In this situation, the focus on the helpee is again underscored by the message "You're in charge here. This interview is for your benefit." At times in later interactions, a somewhat different message may be helpful—for example, "We're both working for your benefit here. I have some expertise in specific helping strategies I want to share with you and teach you." As usual, the use of the nonverbal message depends largely on the helping goal(s), the helpee's responsiveness, and the stage of the helping process.

SUMMARY

We have discussed many aspects of nonverbal communication and their importance in helping. As we've said, it is impossible to *not* communicate nonverbally. Also, we are not always aware of what we *are* communicating. The importance of the helper's nonverbal behavior in helping interactions strongly indicates that helpers must become keenly aware of their nonverbal selves and what they are "saying." While physical appearance may not be changeable, most nonverbal behaviors can be changed or better controlled. The helper must first monitor these behaviors and then work consistently to make them as facilitative as possible for the helping intervention. A balance between complete spontaneity and directed usage of various nonverbal behaviors must be the aim.

THOUGHT QUESTIONS

1. What goals does the helper achieve using effective nonverbal behavior?
2. Is the use of nonverbal behavior in helping a form of manipulation?
3. How is vocal quality a nonverbal behavior?
4. How would your physical appearance affect a helpee on a first meeting?
5. How would your usual style of clothing affect a helpee on a first meeting?
6. In your experience, which nonverbal behavior is the most influential?
7. How could a helper use physical closeness in working with a helpee?
8. How comfortable would you be in touching someone you are helping?
9. How do you react to someone in a uniform?
10. Assume you were to meet with a difficult helpee. List the nonverbal behaviors you would use to facilitate the helpee's disclosure.

4

The Words of Helping: I. Continuing and Leading Responses

Despite the power of a helper's nonverbal behavior to communicate meaning, words *do* matter a great deal. Indeed, perhaps the most basic commonality among different types of helping is the emphasis on words as the medium of help. Historically, as noted in Chapter 1, helping of this kind was referred to as the "talking cure." This remains an apt description, for just as words are the cornerstone of complex human communication, so are they the foundation of the helping process. The basic assumption of helping is a simple one: by discussing personal concerns with a helper, a helpee can learn how to resolve them.

A helper's words can facilitate this process of resolution—or interfere with it. Words *can* help or hurt, contrary to the familiar jingle of children, "Sticks and stones can break my bones, but words can never hurt me." For example, a guilt-ridden person discusses placing her parent in a nursing home.

Helpee: "I've been thinking and thinking and thinking about putting my father in a nursing home. I don't know what's right. Even now, I don't know what's best. He probably will hate it—or hate me. Oh, I don't know what to do!"

A helper can reply in many ways. Some possibilities are:

Helper 1: "Why would you want to do *that* in the first place?"
Helper 2: "Don't worry about it. They'll take good care of him."
Helper 3: "I can see you're very uneasy about placing your father in a home."

Helper 4: "You seem really obsessed with the idea of placing your father in a home."

Put yourself in the role of the helpee. Imagine the way you would feel if these words were spoken to you. Which would help? Which would hurt?

The words of Helper 1 seem most clearly hurtful. They approach sarcasm, particularly if coupled with a brusque tone. Asking "why" tends to put a helpee on the defensive; one message contained in such a "why" question is "You are stupid or foolish for thinking such thoughts." Most of us get up our guard in response to such messages.

The words of Helper 4 also seem rather hurtful. In labeling the helpee's behavior—here, it's labeled as obsessive—the helper acts as judge. These words are evaluative, not understanding. They distract the focus from the helpee's dilemma. The helpee is likely to respond in a threatened manner to the words of this helper.

Least hurtful of all are the words of Helpers 2 and 3, neither of whom judges or threatens. How helpful are they? The words of Helper 2 offer reassurance. They sound sympathetic and they focus on the dilemma, but the truth is that this helpee *is* worried. It is not very helpful to tell a worried person not to worry; rather, it is more helpful to acknowledge that worry.

The words of Helper 3 do just that. Helper 3 recognizes the worry and verbally identifies it, keeping the focus on the dilemma with the emphasis on the *helpee's feelings* about it. These words allow both helpee and helper to go further in exploring those feelings and the bases for them. In all these ways, these words are most helpful.

The purpose of this chapter is to examine different types of verbal helping responses that helpers make and the effects that these responses have on the helping process. Considerable differences exist among various helpers about the value of certain helping responses. Historically, most professionals have stressed the need for helpers to communicate empathy, positive regard, and genuineness in their helping. In fact, Rogers (1957) has suggested that these conditions are *the* necessary and sufficient conditions of helping. He contends that as long as a helper is able to communicate these "core conditions," the helping will be effective. On the other hand, many novice and experienced helpers assume that if they can analyze a person's problem and provide good advice by suggesting what the other person should do, their help will be effective. Consequently, these helpers emphasize the acquisition of additional information about the helpee's problem by asking questions and giving advice based on this new information. We believe that neither orientation is, by itself, correct or incorrect. At certain times, both kinds of orientations are appropriate and desirable. Later in the chapter we will present guidelines for when to use which kind of orientation. First, we will examine different perspectives for understanding verbal responses.

THE CORE CONDITIONS: DEFINITIONS AND FUNCTIONS

Empathy

The central objective of helping is client self-awareness. Thus, the task of the helper is to establish an optimal climate for the facilitation of helpee growth. Empathy is the essential element needed to create a supportive interpersonal environment. According to Rogers (1975), *empathy is a process* rather than a state. More specifically, he defined empathy as:

> entering the private perceptual world of the other and becoming thoroughly at home in it. It involves being sensitive, moment to moment, to the changing felt meanings which flow in this other person, to the fear or rage or tenderness, or confusion, or whatever that he/she is experiencing. It means temporarily living in his/her life, moving about in it delicately without making judgments, sensing meanings of which he/she is scarcely aware, but not trying to uncover feelings of which the person is totally unaware, since this would be too threatening. It includes communicating with your sensing of his/her world as you look with fresh and unfrightened eyes at elements of which the individual is fearful. It means frequently checking with him/her as to the accuracy of your sensings, and being guided by the responses you receive [p. 4].

Furthermore, he notes that empathy is not communicated by a single response or even a series of responses; it is experienced by the helpee throughout an entire helping interaction, through all helper responses, both verbal and nonverbal. The process of empathic communication is therefore quite demanding for helpers. They must put aside their own value system "in order to enter another's world without prejudice" (Rogers, 1975, p. 4). Walt Whitman expressed this idea of total empathy in his poem "Autumn Rivulets":

> There was a child went forth every day,
> And the first object he look'd upon, he became,
> And that object became part of him for that day or a certain part of the day,
> Or for many years or stretching cycles of years....

In helping, total empathy is accepting your helpee's feelings and way of seeing the world as part of yourself.

Empathy, then, implies sensing another's feelings as if they were your own. It is a feeling that you are "with" the helpee. Being able to set aside your own reactions for the present is the key to being empathic. You cannot be "with" your helpee if you are judging the helpee. Nor is being *sympathetic* synonymous with being *empathic*.

Benjamin (1969) notes that sympathy means sharing common feelings, *not* feeling the other's feelings as your own. Suspending both sympathy and judgment is necessary for being "with" the helpee. The "as if" quality of empathy is important, however; *total* empathy implies being nonobjective. *Accurate* empathy, on the other hand, is the ability to suspend judgment *for the moment* while also maintaining a sense of your own separateness. As a helper, you need to be able to step back from total empathy in order to help the helpee examine his or her feelings, assumptions, and expectations.

An apt example occurred with a helpee of one of the authors. This woman related to the helper an incident which disgusted and horrified her—as well as him—and involved the thoughtless killing of a pet by a neighbor. The helpee went on to describe how she handled the ensuing encounters with the animal's owners and with neighbors. It would have been easiest, in this situation, for the helper to sympathize with the horror of the killing by saying: "What a terrible thing to do! How cruel . . . . You must have felt awful." These responses, however, would not have been particularly helpful coming from a helper; from a friend, sympathy is fine. Rather, the helper focused first on the helpee's immediate feelings and then on her feelings about how she handled the encounters: "This killing made you very angry, as well as disgusted. But you were pleased that you were able to express your anger in a controlled way." The helpee's purpose in relating the incident was not to gain sympathy but to point out a change in her behavior of which she was proud. Accurate empathy allowed the helper to feel that pride and focus on it for the purpose of assisting the helpee in examining her own feelings and expectations about the expression of anger.

Genuineness

According to helpers whose philosophies involve facilitating helpee self-growth as a major goal, the helper must be spontaneous and self-disclosing. In this model, genuine helpers express directly what they are experiencing. Spontaneity gives a sense of immediacy to the helping relationship, a sense of "here-and-now" feelings. Good helpers are real and authentic during helping, openly expressing their feelings to helpees even when they are somewhat negative. When a helpee talked with difficulty about her fears of having a progressively debilitating disease, the helper involved wanted to reach out to the helpee. She said, "I feel your pain and fear as you talk about this possibility. And I'm frightened for you. I feel protective at this moment, too. I'd like to hug you." The helper was candid about her feelings. Moreover, the feelings expressed were right then and there, in the immediate situation.

Such openness serves as a model to the helpee. By being willing to discuss personal feelings, the helper encourages the helpee to respond similarly. The helpee opens up and learns to be genuine, too. The helpee mentioned just above seemed to respond directly to her helper's genuineness. In the next helping session, the helpee began to discuss feelings and incidents about which she had previously been very reticent. In addition, sometime shortly thereafter, the helpee was able to tell the helper that a particular comment the helper had made hurt her to hear. The two were then able to examine what that was about. The helping relationship was thus directly engaged as a tool in the helping process, because both helper and helpee were being genuine.

An atmosphere of personal sharing is created. The helper's genuineness also prevents the helpee from becoming defensive during the helping relationship because both helpee and helper know that the ongoing relationship will be an honest one. Genuineness, like empathy, is perceived to be a process and not a state. It is continuous, not static; continuing openness and authenticity mark the process.

Unconditional Positive Regard

A basic tenet held by many helpers is that they must be caring in order to help. This caring, often considered respect, is the ability to accept the helpee's behavior without destructive evaluation. Respect is the willingness to be "with" your helpees and to be concerned about their welfare—to respect their uniqueness and to respect their need for self-determination. Helpers, then, accept helpees' rights to have feelings, goals, and needs that might be different from their own.

For example, one helpee was working toward defining his identity after having been severely depressed for a long period of time. He expressed two main interests to the helper: the first goal was to return to school for an advanced degree; the second goal was to find a job without the degree. The helper's own identity needs included intellectual recognition and achievement. The goal of studying for an advanced degree would be more satisfying to those needs than would a job. However, the helpee's needs for intellectual achievement were not as strong, though he much desired recognition. Through the helping interaction, it became clear that he believed a job would provide him with some recognition and would also meet other needs (for example, financial autonomy toward greater self-reliance). Ultimately, the helpee chose to seek a job and not return to school. The helper's role here was to respect the helpee's self-determination by assisting him in exploring his options and the feelings involved without imposing her own needs.

There are different ways to think about this issue. Thoreau suggested that each person steps to the beat of a different drummer and must listen to her or his own drummer. From a slightly different perspective, one can take the view that one's actions are strange only insofar as they are labeled "strange" by others; self-labeling may result in their being seen as perfectly natural. This is not to say that helpers always agree with the helpee's feelings and goals, but they can respect them in the helpee, can listen to them, and can respond empathically without judging their rightness or goodness. To work on more effective goals and feelings, the helper might say how he or she views things differently but should not deny, negate, or reject the helpee's own goals and feelings.

A more complicated example than that above involved a different helpee. This helpee worked in a factory some distance from her home, and the shift she worked took her away from home from mid-afternoon through midnight. In addition, her working days rotated weekly so there was little predictability to her schedule. Her husband's schedule was more consistent, though it too had unanticipated shifts. By and large, however, his main duties involved the hours of a regular workday. Both became increasingly distressed by their lack of time together. Even on common days off, when they occurred, one or both found themselves too tired or too drained to be able to be companionable. In viewing alternatives, it was clear that the woman had greater flexibility. She could seek a different position which would decrease travel time immensely and give the two of them a bit more time together. Alternatively, she could seek day-shift hours, either at her current job or at a new position. It was clear to the helper that much stress would be alleviated by a job change of some sort. The helpee's own needs would have been best met by increasing time with her spouse and by decreasing the "out-of-sync" hours of work so that a more usual range of activities could be followed. These needs were shared by the helpee, but the helpee's feelings about them differed as did her goals. The helper listened without evaluation, but disagreed with the helpee's choice to remain where she was. The disagreement was based on observed behavioral and feeling effects of tension related to the location and work hours. The helper believed it important to note this, without negating or rejecting the helpee's point of view at that time or in ensuing discussions. As with empathy and genuineness, unconditional positive regard is a process.

Problems with the Core Conditions Model

There are some basic weaknesses in the core conditions model of helping. For example, empathy implies that the helper is able to enter the world of another, experiencing life as the helpee experiences it and suspending judgment and bias. But can we *truly* know how someone else feels? Unless we have experienced all the situations another individual has, we may understand something about how someone else feels but we may not truly experience an event or feeling exactly as he or she would. For example, women as a group have experienced discrimination but may not really understand discrimination as encountered by Blacks. Middle-class Blacks do not experience discrimination as poor Blacks do. Furthermore, even one poor Black is probably unable to understand *exactly* how another poor Black reacts to discrimination. Indeed, all of us have unique experiences which prevent us from totally entering into someone else's world. We may approximate someone else's experience but we cannot have it. This difference may be important in helping. It may be more valuable to *try* to understand another and communicate your *trying* instead of attempting to understand completely. When a client worried that she was falling victim to multiple sclerosis, the helper involved could not *truly* experience the fear and despair, but could convey that she was in touch with it and recognized those feelings of the helpee. Responding to helpees with a slightly different understanding of a situation may enable helpees to clarify their situation and feelings. This clarification may lead to a deeper understanding of the situation. With multiple sclerosis, the helpee saw no hope of engaging in a meaningful life. The helper, on the other hand, was able to facilitate a better differentiated examination of possibilities and impossibilities, which encouraged the helpee to a different perception of her life with more positive feelings, despite the fear—and the anger. Being somewhat accurate in identifying how a helpee feels, then, may be more effective than a total understanding of another's feelings. And trying may lead to actually feeling many of the feelings due to suspended judgment (just as in Chapter 3 it was noted that a nonverbal demonstration of interest often leads to feeling interested).

Contradictions exist not only about the value of empathy *per se*, but also about the validity of exhibiting all three core conditions simultaneously. Can one be genuine and have unconditional respect at the same time? Maybe some of us can, but not all of us. For example, a male helpee comes to a female helper and says "How can you help me? You're inferior! You should be back in the kitchen. The thought of it, a woman trying to help *me*!" Is it possible for this helper to respect him and yet tell him how she feels? Would she still be able to be empathic and caring toward him after hearing his attitude toward her? Perhaps; perhaps not. Reread the descriptions of the core conditions and place yourself in this situation or a similar one.

A final and most important problem with the core conditions model is that it does not identify specific words a helper needs to use, except for empathy which calls for a focus on feelings. But how is a helper to be "genuine"? How is a helper to express "unconditional positive regard"? Unless the specific words that connote these concepts can be described in examples, helpers will find it very difficult to create the core conditions. The major helping in a helping relationship is effected through verbal expression. The perspective we take addresses this problem by proposing a set of discrete types of verbal responses, each with specific kinds of phrasing and types of words. If helpers use these responses well, they can create a helping atmosphere in which they are perceived as empathic, genuine, and showing unconditional positive regard. The remainder of this chapter will focus on two major types of verbal responses—*continuing responses* and *leading responses*. A third type of response, *self-referent responses,* will be discussed in the following chapter.

CONTINUING RESPONSES

Put yourself in the role of a person seeking help. You may be discouraged by your life situation and you'd like to talk about it with someone who will listen. You're not sure what will help you, but you'd like someone who is understanding and who is a good listener. Basically you want someone *you can talk to.* The helper has similar goals for new helpees: to listen to and understand what's troubling them. Helpers must first listen and then later try to help resolve the problem. Before a problem can be tackled, it must be identified and defined in depth. Continuing responses are designed to meet the needs of helper and helpee. These responses help the helpee to feel "heard" and "understood," and they provide the helper with a powerful tool for understanding the helpee.

Continuing responses are essential to establishing effective communication between helper and helpee. Generally, the helper's role in initial interactions is that of a *facilitator.* Especially when meeting with a helpee for the first time, the helper must encourage the helpee to talk. The helper's goal is to allow helpees to present their concern in a nonthreatening, supportive interpersonal environment. Helpers, then, are nondirective in that their responses are intended to disinhibit the common reluctance of the helpee to discuss troubling personal concerns. Helpers' responses should convey that they are sincerely interested and that they are listening. This builds a sense of trust. The effort is giving an important message: *the helper is trying to understand.* Continuing responses, by conveying understanding, should also increase the helpee's self-disclosure and self-exploration. Additionally, continuing responses serve to clarify both to the helper and to the helpee what is being said. They aid the helper in checking out the helpee's feelings and situation, and they aid the helpee to rethink or review what has been expressed so far. In sum, effective continuing responses should facilitate helpees talking more personally, disclosing their feelings more openly, and relating their "here-and-now" feelings. Continuing responses generally promote the helpee's *continuing to talk.* There are two types of continuing responses: *content* and *affective.*

Content Responses

A content response summarizes the substance of what the helpee has said. A content response underscores the important content of a helpee's message. It may highlight through summary the prior statement only, several statements in the total interaction, or the whole interaction. An example of highlighting the substance of the prior statement only is:

Helpee: "I just don't know what to do anymore. Nothing I do seems like fun. I moved here three months ago and all I've felt is blah."

Helper: "Moving here has been stressful for you."

A content response highlighting several statements would be:

Helpee: "My work is getting to me. I work all the time, though I said to myself I wouldn't become a workaholic. And now look at me! I've been really rundown lately. Not only that, I get pains in my chest. I just keep on plugging away, but I get more and more tense."

Helper: "You believe the tension you've been experiencing results from your constant working and getting rundown."

It is not possible here to give an example of an entire interaction in dialogue. For the sake of illustration, let's assume that an hour's discussion between helper and helpee has just taken place, starting and ending with the following helpee statements.

Helpee: (First statement) "I'm not sure where to begin today. So many things have happened this week, and I'm feeling really good about them: my new car, my relationship with this girl I met, how I get along with my parents...."

Helpee: (Last statement) "I guess I've really grown a lot. That feels good!"

Helper: "To summarize, you've recognized many positive changes in yourself and this week you've seen them influence the ways you handle important relationships in your life, as well as formerly difficult situations—like deciding about a new car."

Thus, such a content response is most often a *summary statement,* pulling together the highlights of the helping interaction.

Content responses are designed to encourage helpees to continue talking about the topic itself. Their purpose is to draw them out and help them elaborate. If content responses are made effectively, helpees talk more about the topic, disclosing more information about the important elements of the topic.

Effective content responses are not simple restatements or "echoic reflections" of the helpee's statement. Rather, they paraphrase and bring together into one thought a number of statements that the helpee has made. They spotlight what the helpee has said. In so doing, content responses allow the *helpee* to hear what he or she has just said, which encourages the helpee to think more about the problem or issue. One helpee's experience in just that was as follows. He had been talking about how tired he was of having to deal with his parents and how he would like to just obliterate the problem by moving to a distant state.

Helpee: "If I moved, I'd never have to speak to them again. Wouldn't that be a treat! It's such a pain."

Helper: "You're thinking about setting up your life in a way that will completely cut off your relationship with your parents."

Helpee: "Well—I don't mean *completely*. I don't see how anyone could break away completely. I guess I didn't mean I *wouldn't* speak to them again, but I wouldn't have these frequent visits I always feel obligated to make."

Helper: "It's the responsibility you feel toward them that you believe you can shift by moving."

Helpee: "Yes, that's it really. But I don't know if that's really true. I'd still feel it."

Helper: "You don't believe that moving would resolve those strong feelings."

Helpee: "No, I don't think it would. Maybe we should talk about my feelings of responsibility, then."

Thus, the helpee was assisted in getting to a useful point of exploration by the helper's skillful use of content responses. The content responses allowed the helpee to see what he had really said and to rethink whether it was what he truly meant. In this instance it was not, and so the helper's content responses helped to clarify what the helpee did and did not mean.

Because of the clarification function, helpers themselves learn a great deal about their helpees by using content responses, more than they learn by simply questioning the helpee. Questions often elicit defensiveness, especially early on in a helping relationship and especially if they are asked one after the other. Content responses are silent "prods" that elicit information without causing defensiveness. At various points, the helper may want to summarize what has gone on to enable the helpee to examine it more closely. By allowing the helpee to hear what he or she has just said, the helper promotes a deeper search by the helpee into his or her perspective on the topic.

It is possible at times to formulate content responses in the form of a question if the helper is seeking very specific feedback about what a helpee is saying. For example, a helper could begin a content response with such introductory phrases as: "Are you saying...?" or "Do you mean that...?" For example:

Helpee: "I'm not sure I'll be able to make next week's session. I've got so much to do to get ready for the move."
Helper: "Are you saying that you cannot schedule an appointment?"

Such responses are content responses *only* if they attempt to summarize what the helpee has already stated and do not seek additional information. However, beginning content responses with a question should be done sparingly since it often communicates helper confusion and uncertainty.

Some examples of content responses to simple helpee statements are:

1. *Helpee:* "What a miserable day. My car broke down, my dog got away, and I lost my wallet. What'll happen next?"
   Helper: "You've really been hit a lot today."
2. *Helpee:* "My father was just laughing and laughing when he heard I made it into a college."
   Helper: "You see your father as greeting your acceptance at a college with amusement."
3. *Helpee:* "Do you know what kind of person I am? Wouldn't you like to know?"
   Helper: "You wonder if I'd really like to know the real you."

While reading the following interactions, consider the alternative responses. Which one in each set is the most effective content response?

4. *Helpee:* "I really have trouble with my temper. I just fume when someone says something I disagree with. It drives me up a wall."
   Helper: a. "It drives you up a wall to hear someone you disagree with."
   b. "Disagreements make you boil."
   c. "You fume when someone counters your opinion."

Any of these responses are possible content responses. Each of them contains elements of the helpee's statement. Response (a), though, uses the helpee's own words a bit too closely to be most effective. Response (c) may not be fully accurate since perhaps the helpee meant only that hearing a different opinion was problem enough and was not really ready to discuss actual confrontations. Response (b), then, may be the most effective at this time. It's a simple paraphrase of the helpee's statement and yet offers substance which the helpee can elaborate on and further clarify.

5. *Helpee:* "My needs to be a helper stem to some extent from my belligerence to society in general. I want to help those who are exploited. I need to feel important."

   Helper:
   a. "Your belligerence to society leads you to want to assist others in their problems."
   b. "Helping will allow you to feel important yourself in the role you play in society."
   c. "Do you mean that you need to be and be seen as *useful* in a social sense, to do something good in society?"

Statement (a) again seems too close a restatement of the helpee's words and it does not carry the significant content to the helpee's attention. Statement (b) highlights the significant content but may too closely follow the helpee's words. Statement (c) highlights the significant content without using the helpee's words. It is a useful clarification of the content.

Affective Responses

In helping others, it is not enough to hear helpees' actual words. They tell only part of the story. Helpers must also hear between the words; they must "hear" the feelings helpees are experiencing. Remember how much meaning is communicated nonverbally. Two helpees may say the *same* words in vastly different ways, thus revealing very different feelings about their situation. No two people respond alike to similar situations. Two executives seeking a promotion in their firm may both say to their spouses "I didn't make it." One may say it in a matter-of-fact fashion; the other may say it with a tremor in his or her voice. These differences in how they spoke the very same words indicate that each has different feelings about the situation—and thus somewhat different concerns. To discover what a person's concern *really* is entails listening for feelings and labeling them. Think about the two executives. What might their different feelings be? their concerns?

Listening for feelings rather than solely for ideas is a crucial helping skill. Feelings about one's ideas and situation are a good deal of the substance of each person's existence. As Aesop says, "Beware that you do not lose the whole substance by grasping at the shadow." Skilled helpers aim at exploring the substance of a problem or concern, and attempt to identify core feelings and meaning. When we are upset or distraught, it is greatly comforting to talk with someone who is perceptive enough to hear beyond our words and who is able to read feeling signals. A helpee of one of the authors said this outright. He had recently moved to town and was terribly unhappy. In listening to him recount his travails, the following exchange occurred:

Helpee: "I'm so miserable. Nothing pleases me. I don't like the town. There's no shopping, not like in the city. My wife can't even buy my kids decent clothes, the choices are so limited. Well, they're decent but very few choices. I guess I'll get used to it.... And the schools—I don't really know how good they are, but we had our hearts set on a private school. And what's here? Just an elementary school. Which reminds me: nothing seems as good as home."

Helper: "You're feeling very trapped."

Helpee: "*Yes I am.* I don't feel like there's any way to turn. At least in the city, I had choices—even if I didn't always use them. Trapped—yeah. You know, you're right. Other people keep reassuring me or trying to comfort me. Saying "You'll get used to it" or "Things aren't so bad as they seem." That just doesn't make me feel better. Even if I *do* get used to it, that's not what I'm feeling now. You hit it right on the head."

Helpers can demonstrate empathy by using *affective responses*. Affective responses identify feelings, especially feelings which the helpee has not yet labeled. Many times people do not label their feelings. Making affective responses is a difficult task because the helper must pinpoint the feelings *within* what a helpee says, as in the example above. The helpee never said he felt trapped or even stifled. That is, he didn't say it *directly*. His choice of words and the rush of words said it. It is not only *what* is said but *how* it is said that must be considered. Helpees' feelings can be inferred from their nonverbal behavior. Feeling signals are largely nonverbal, and tonal quality is especially telling. It is particularly important to be alert to feelings suggested by *incongruencies* between a helpee's nonverbal behaviors and the words used. Consider a helpee who says with a smile on his face, "I was really scared. I was petrified." A smile seems inconsistent with such words.

The helper must ask "What may this helpee be saying about the experience of being scared? His nonverbal behavior just doesn't match the verbal." An empathic helper might follow this helpee's statement with the following response.

Helper: "The experience was frightening, but at the same time exhilarating in some way."

That is, the incongruency between the helpee's words and nonverbal expression suggested as yet unlabeled feelings. It was important for the helper to read that feeling signal and identify it in an affective response. This paves the way for the helpee to explore his or her mixed responses in difficult or life-threatening situations and to examine how constructive such reactions are. The helper's alertness to unexpressed feelings often opens the door.

Affective responses often begin with the phrase "You are feeling" followed by an affective word. For instance:

Helpee: "I'd like to make the right decision. But I keep asking myself just what is right for me?"
Helper: "You're feeling puzzled right now."

Often, content responses are mistaken for affective responses, especially if they begin with "You feel." It is important to remember this rule: If "think" or "believe" can be substituted for the word "feel" in a response and not lose the meaning, it is *not* an affective response. "You feel your parents are too critical of you" is a content response. This is a thought or a belief, not a feeling. The appropriate phrasing is "You believe your parents are too critical of you." Nor is it an affective response if the word "that" follows the word "feel." For example, "You feel that it will be hard for you" is not an affective response. The appropriate phrasing is "You think it will be hard for you." If an affective response is preferable, the helper might say "You're worried that it will be too hard for you." Some examples of affective responses are:

1. *Helpee:* "My girl left town yesterday. I really struck out with her. We just couldn't get together on anything."
   Helper: "You're sad that she's gone."
2. *Helpee:* "I got really nervous when he came in. I'd wanted to meet him for two years."
   Helper: "When you saw him, you were feeling really excited."
3. *Helpee:* "I'm tired of taking it all the time. I never get things my way."

Helper: "Never getting your way makes you resentful."

While reading the following interactions, consider the alternative responses as you did earlier. Which seems the best affective response?

4. *Helpee:* "My son is a great kid. He's fun to be with. I'm really glad we decided to have kids."
   Helper: a. "You're proud of your son and enjoy being with him."
   b. "You think your son is terrific."
   c. "You're pleased with being a father."

When you read these helper responses, you noted that statement (b) is not an affective response at all, but instead is a content response. How accurately does (c) identify those feelings expressed right there in the helpee's statement? It seems to pinpoint a likely feeling, but it goes beyond the immediate "data." It may be just a bit early to infer that particular feeling; the helper needs to wait to hear what the helpee says next. Statement (a), however, identifies the main feelings suggested in the helpee's words. These feelings are important to empathize with first. They are feelings the helpee is bursting with and wants to talk about.

5. *Helpee:* "I've been putting myself down lately. I think it's because I see myself always giving in to my friends and not saying what I really want."
   Helper: a. "You're pretty depressed."
   b. "Giving in to your friends makes you angry."
   c. "You're disappointed in yourself for not being more assertive with your friends, and you'd like to be able to say what you want."

Let's examine these responses. All are affective responses. Not all are on target, however. Statement (a) seems to miss the boat: the helpee used the word "down" but was not talking about a general feeling; rather, the helpee was pinpointing a specific area of concern that statement (a) does not identify. Statement (b) acknowledges that specific area of concern but does not seem to accurately identify the feeling expressed by the helpee at this time. Both the concern and the main feeling are identified in statement (c). Being "down on oneself" suggests disappointment. In addition, statement (c) labels another feeling—the desire to be assertive. Both significant feelings are thus labeled in statement (c), which is the most accurate affective response in this set of alternatives.

Further Pointers on Continuing Response Usage

Facilitative affective responses do not repeat the same or similar feeling words every time. Beginning helpers often use a narrow affective vocabulary; words like sad, mad, glad are heard repeatedly. An effective helper needs to build a wide affective vocabulary. Reviewing special affective vocabulary lists is one strategy. Listening for the variety of feeling words used by others is a second strategy. Being alert to words used in films, on television, in novels, and in songs is yet another source of enriching your own affective vocabulary. It takes some effort and concentration: tuning in to feelings is the key.

Effective helpers try to pinpoint and integrate for the helpee a number of feelings as expressed or implied from several aspects of an interaction. Identifying the feelings being expressed is the first step. The second is to select one or two affective words which best describe the feelings. Being able to label the feelings differentially is an important skill; having a broad affective vocabulary facilitates this skill. For example:

Helpee: (Spoken in clipped tones) "It drives me crazy when my wife interrupts me. I just can't stand it."

Helper: "Being interrupted is very irritating to you. When your wife does so, you feel very angry and beside yourself with fury."

It is also useful for the helper to compare and contrast the feelings the helpee has from various points within an interaction. One woman helpee, for instance, was discussing her need for support from members of the family. She talked first about approaching her husband.

Helpee: (Spoken quickly, with some quavering in her voice) "My husband just refused to listen. He just doesn't seem to care. I don't know—it doesn't matter to him that I'm in need."

Helper: "You're downcast that your husband was so unresponsive."

Helpee: (Spoken in brusque tones) "Yes. It made me pretty upset. And then my sister. She listened, but she didn't want to give me anything. She pretty much said to me that I had to face being on my own."

Helper: "You felt rejected again—first your husband and then your sister disappointed you."

Helpee: (Spoken in sharp tones, with some tearginess in her eyes) "Not rejected—angry. I was angry that he wouldn't give me any support. I thought he of all people would be willing to."

Helper: "It made you mad to be refused. At the same time, you're feeling abandoned by your family. It's deeply upsetting, and it hurts."

Comparison of feelings from various interactions is also valuable. For instance, a helper might respond: "It seems as if you may be feeling confused. Last week you were upset about the situation while this week you seem to be resigned to its consequences." The more the helper is able to integrate and compare feelings, the more he or she will further the helpee's exploration, clarification, and understanding. Helpers do not add their own feelings into their responses: an affective response identifies and labels the feelings of the helpee only!

In the same way, affective responses label the helpee's feelings, *not* the feelings of others the helpee is discussing. Spotlighting the helpee is the key. Which is the appropriate response in the following interaction?

Helpee: "My friend made me so angry. He said he was going to be there at the party, and then he didn't show up. Later he said he was really sorry: he'd intended to go, but got stuck doing something else."

Helper: a. "Although he intended to come, he couldn't and felt sorry about it."
b. "Although your friend apologized, you still feel mad and hurt."

Statement (b) is the appropriate affective response; it identifies the helpee's feelings about the friend's behavior. Statement (a) is inappropriate; it identifies what the helpee said about the friend and focuses attention on the friend's feeling. Helper and helpee cannot explore another's feelings; they can explore what *the helpee* perceives and feels about another person. The focus must be on the helpee.

Both content and affective responses are designed to enable helpees to continue to talk and examine their situation. The intention of these responses is not to close off any area of concern the helpee may have but to facilitate the examination of a variety of concerns and feelings and to clarify them. Research demonstrates that affective responses elicit the most talk about feelings and the greatest degree of talking *per se* by the helpee. These responses are thus very powerful and should be used liberally throughout the helping process.

Continuing responses, both affective and content, are probably used most frequently in the Entry (Stage 1), Exploration (Stage 2), and Clarification (Stage 3) Stages of the helping process (see Chapter 1). However, they should be considered the responses of choice *whenever the helper's goal is to facilitate discussion*. Since they ensure the flow of conversation, they should be adopted as the ordinary conversational style of helping. In other words, the helper should have a convincing reason for using other responses that should relate to the specific goals the helper has in making the response—goals relating to the purpose and direction of helping at that moment and overall.

LEADING RESPONSES

Continuing responses help the helper to understand the helpee's situation. But is understanding enough? The history of helping consists of contrasting answers to this question, and it is likely that the answer will always remain elusive. As we have stated earlier, helping involves addressing the issue of change for helpees. After the problem or issue is understood in depth, the helper and helpee must question whether or not some change is necessary. Since change will be needed for many helpees, helpers must have verbal tools for designing change plans. Leading responses serve this general purpose. Leading responses are those responses which have the effect of directing or redirecting a helpee's thinking. *Questioning responses* come into this category, as do *influencing responses* and *advice-giving responses*.

Questions

The question response has received minimal attention in the helping literature even though it is the response that many helpers, especially novice helpers, most often make. Some professionals have little regard for questions because they are not considered to demonstrate empathy. The major danger of using questions is that the helping interaction may become a question-and-answer period in which the helpee becomes passive. It is vital to promote the helpee's very active participation in the helping process.

Experienced helpers use questions to provoke new insights. Questioning responses help the helpee to consider a new area for exploration. While we have noted earlier that some content and affective responses may be grammatical questions, they are usually not designed to provoke a completely new focus, so they are mainly ways of identifying what the helpee has already said or implied. The questioning response, on the other hand, is generally not used to clarify what has been said but is used to move the interaction in a new direction. Helpers ask questions to enable helpees to provide additional information from within themselves. There are two kinds of questions: closed and open.

Closed questions are almost always answered by a *yes* or a *no* response or at most with a two or three word answer. Some examples of closed questions are:

1. "Did you like that?"
2. "Were you angry?"
3. "When did that start?"
4. "Did you have fun at the party?"

There may be some situations in which closed questions are useful. For instance, at times when the helper must learn some factual information from the helpee for record-keeping, a closed question might be appropriate: for example, "What grade did you complete?" Or, when seeking to understand the social context of the helpee's life, an occasional closed question might be appropriate: for example, "How many brothers and sisters do you have?"

Closed questions, however, should be avoided since they restrict the helpee to answering in a very specific way. Consider the following alternate dialogues.

Dialogue 1
Helpee 1: "I've been wanting to apply to college for a while, but I haven't yet."
Helper 1: "Are you worried?"
Helpee 1: "No, I'm not."
Helper 1: "Are you scared?"
Helpee 1: "Maybe I am."

Dialogue 2
Helpee 1: "I've been wanting to apply to college for a while, but I haven't yet."
Helper 2: "You're hesitant about applying."
Helpee 1: "Yes, really, I'm reluctant to put myself on the line I guess. I'm a bit scared."
Helper 2: "Taking that risk scares you. What expectations do you have about applying?"
Helpee 1: "That's just it. I'm not sure what to expect. It all seems so vague—what the criteria are, I mean. I'm not sure I'll measure up, even though my grades are pretty good and I did well on the entrance exams. I suppose I expect all the other applicants to have done even better. And then, even if I get accepted, I worry that I won't be able to compete."

In Dialogue 1, the helpee responded tersely, with few words. In Dialogue 2, the helpee was much more vocal about his thoughts and feelings. What made the difference? To a great extent, the difference was due to the use of closed questions in Dialogue 1 and the subsequent avoidance of such questions in Dialogue 2. The closed questions in the first dialogue gave the helpee little leeway in responding. The helpee essentially had to follow the helper's lead and was restricted in range of response because the form of question used—closed—elicits limited answers.

On the other hand, the helpee's range of response was unrestricted in Dialogue 2. The helper used a continuing response first—in this case, an affective response—which facilitated the helpee's own revelation of being scared. After acknowledging that fear, the helper used a questioning response—an open question—which allowed the helpee to explore this new area (expectations) without prematurely closing the door. Another problem with closed questions is that they often impose a helper's viewpoint or area of interest on the helpee and lead the helpee away from his or her focus. This is illustrated in the interchange below.

Helpee: "I've been having trouble studying lately. Just can't seem to keep my mind on it."
Helper: "Do you usually enjoy studying?"
Helpee: "I don't know. Enjoy?"
Helper: "Do you usually get into it?"
Helpee: "I guess so."
Helper: "So you can study when you want to. Do you study now by yourself?"
Helpee: "Yes."
Helper: "Do you keep a radio on?"
Helpee: "No."
Helper: "Is your roommate around when you study?"
Helpee: "Sometimes. I don't see what you're getting at."
Helper: "I thought your study situation might be the trouble. But it doesn't seem to be."

What happened in this interaction? The helper seemed to become confused and a bit impatient. Rather than exploring the helpee's direct concern—her recent restlessness about studying—the helper led the helpee to examine the physical set-up for studying. By using questions instead of continuing responses, the helper ignored the feelings of the helpee. By using *closed* questions, the helper prematurely shut the door on exploration and took the helpee away from her focus. Instead, as the helper says at the end of the exchange, he *thought* the physical situation might be relevant. The truth is it may be! But it was an inappropriate lead for the time, as neither helper nor helpee had a clear understanding of the concern. Moreover, the closed questions did not allow the helpee to move back to *her* focus. The effect of the closed questions was to maintain the focus on the *helper's* hunch.

In contrast to closed questions, *open questions* foster communication since they cannot be answered with a single word. Some examples of open questions are:

1. "How do you feel?"
2. "What did you do then?"
3. "How might you tackle that?"
4. "What ideas do you have about that?"
5. "What feelings were aroused in that situation?"

Open questions give helpees freedom to respond and to describe their situation. Research has shown that open questions elicit more affective speech than do closed questions. Because of this, they are much more effective than closed questions. While allowing the helpee to suggest his or her own feelings and viewpoint, they also provide much more information than closed questions. For example, when one helpee was ready for setting goals and exploring options for attaining them, some of the initial helping dialogue went like this:

Helper: "We have reached the point where you seem eager to *do* something different for yourself."
Helpee: "I really do want to change things. I wasn't sure before if I could, but now I'd sure like to try."
Helper: "You feel committed to making some changes in your behaviors now."
Helpee: "Absolutely. I know I need to, and I know I want to."
Helper: "What are some of those changes?"
Helpee: "Well, I haven't given it a lot of thought yet. I do believe one thing I need to learn is how to deal with anger better than I do."
Helper: "What happens when you get angry?"
Helpee: "I get hysterical, and I don't like it. I get disgusted with myself and just explode in a rage."
Helper: "What do you actually do in this rage?"
Helpee: "I scream and yell and rant on and on. I call the other person names and make sarcastic remarks. I really attack. Oh, I hate it!"
Helper: "Then, your general goal is to learn how to handle angry feelings in a constructive way rather than an attacking way. Specific goals include stopping the screaming and stopping the sarcasm. To do so, another goal is to find alternative responses with which to express anger. You said there were other changes. What are some of those?"

Through the use of several appropriately timed open questions, the helper assisted the helpee to examine and set initial goals for change. The helper did not suggest those goals, but rather allowed the helpee to do so. What the helpee did was to set the initial direction for exploration by asking, "What are some of those changes?" By using other open questions, the helper encouraged the helpee to be more concrete about the changes without imposing a particular set of changes on the helpee. Thus, much information was elicited, about both specific changes and feelings.

There are other forms of questions aside from closed questions that are of dubious value. "Why" questions should especially be avoided. "Why do you feel that way?" or "Why do you want to change your major?" seem reasonable enough on the surface. In many interchanges between friends, such questions get asked frequently. Recall how you feel, though, when a friend or parent or teacher asks you "Why?" Most likely you recognize feelings of defensiveness. Your guard goes up. "Why" questions tend to elicit justifications rather than explorations. Even a question like "What made you do that?" is problematic; it may be a disguised "Why did you do that?" and should be avoided. When helpees feel threatened, the helping relationship is less effective. Avoiding frequent questions and especially avoiding "why" questions is crucial to effective helping.

Unfortunately, questions are often thought to be necessary and efficient. This is especially so when new, specific information is needed, as in an initial interview between a physician and patient. In fact, however, the use of questions can be inefficient. If helpers sense the answer to the questions they are asking, or if they think they know the answer, they can make continuing responses instead. To see whether you know the answer to a question you are about to ask, first ask it silently to yourself and try to answer for the helpee. If you can, respond with a *continuing response*. Often, using a *tentative* introduction such as "It seems as if you're feeling" will be more effective in furthering exploration and simultaneously demonstrating empathy than a question—even an open one—that you might otherwise have asked. Thus, while some open questions may be appropriate in the early stages of Exploration (Stage 2) and Clarification (Stage 3), they are usually less appropriate than an affective response. In later stages, questions become more useful.

Influencing

Particularly when the helping relationship has progressed to the action-oriented stages—Integration (Stage 4), Program Planning (Stage 5), Action-Taking (Stage 6), and Reviewing (Stage 7)—the helper needs tools to assist the helpee in going forward with change. Influencing responses are used to promote change in the attitudes and beliefs of the helpee; they *indirectly* encourage behavior change.

An influencing response is the helper's opinion about an idea or an attitude which the helpee has expressed; for example, "I think your idea about seeing a doctor to check out the dizziness you experienced is very worthwhile." Through such an influencing response, the helper adds emphasis to the helpee's own thinking about a particular set of beliefs or actions. Thus, influencing responses focus on topics previously discussed by the helpee. No new solution to the problem is offered; rather, influencing responses are intended to follow up an idea or way of looking at a problem that the helpee has initiated. Other examples are:

1. *Helpee:* "I've been considering buying a new house, but I swing back and forth about the wisdom of doing so when I think about the advantages and disadvantages."
   Helper: "Carefully considering the pros and cons is a useful approach."
2. *Helpee:* "I used to think that my parents were trying to impose their values on me. Now I think what they were doing was not that so much as letting me know what they thought."
   Helper: "Looking at their behavior in a more positive light is helpful."
3. *Helpee:* "I was thinking about flying to California, but I'm worried about flying after the recent newspaper stories about crashes."
   Helper: "It's unlikely that the plane would crash."

The main goal of using influencing responses is to positively reinforce or negatively reinforce the helpee's idea or attitude. It is partly through such influence that the helpee further considers those ideas and related actions. Using an influencing response is one helpful way of guiding the helpee to take major responsibility for his or her own changes.

If positive reinforcement is desirable, the influencing response is formulated *to encourage* the helpee to follow through on the idea.

1. *Helpee:* "I was offered some new dope. It might really be great, but I'm not going to touch the stuff."
   Helper: "It's very wise to avoid using dope."
2. *Helpee:* "When I got anxious I began to wonder if I should see a psychologist."
   Helper: "Taking that first step to deal with your anxiety is very sensible."
3. *Helpee:* "I really ought to respond differently to my husband when he's upset. He never says so, just makes certain looks or noises. That usually makes me angry, and I

                    lash out at him. What I need to do is overlook those things and let him know I see he is upset."
Helper: "Acknowledging his distress instead of ignoring it will be most beneficial."

In these examples, the helper attempts to positively influence the helpee's own approach. The helper's statements focused on the idea or action expressed by the helpee and used positive evaluation terms to suggest encouragement.

If negative reinforcement is desirable, the influencing response is formulated to *discourage* the helpee from following through on an idea or action.

1. *Helpee:*   "I've been thinking about taking a new job although I've only been at this one for two months."
   Helper: "Taking a new job so soon seems like a questionable idea."
2. *Helpee:*   "I didn't want to think so, but I'm certain my aunt purposely put my cousin up to it just to annoy me."
   Helper: "From what you said, I believe you're wrong in your conclusion."
3. *Helpee:*   "I'm just going to go out and file for a divorce before my husband gets back."
   Helper: "Rushing into a divorce may be extra painful."

In these examples, the helper attempts to influence the helpee to reconsider, to examine a different viewpoint, or to defer taking action. The helper believes the ideas professed by the helpee are counterproductive and therefore wishes to discourage the helpee from following up on them. Mildly negative evaluative terms are used to do so.

Sometimes helpers make responses which are of an interpretive nature. Such responses begin with attitudes or ideas which the helpee has expressed but offer some additional perspective from the helper's viewpoint. For instance:

Helpee: "No one really likes me. It's because I'm fat. If I were slim, I'd have lots of dates."
Helper: "Maybe it's not only your weight that's the problem."

In this statement, the helper interprets the helpee's problem with an influencing response. The response is intended to spark the helpee's thinking about other aspects of the dilemma, ways in which people may be distanced other than by the weight problem. Such responses are generally made by more experienced helpers who have a finely honed sense of timing and phrasing. Interpretive responses, while influencing, can be challenging or even threatening. Newer helpers are better off using clearer positive and negative influencing responses when appropriate and avoiding interpretive types of constructions.

Influencing responses used as leading responses reflect the *helper's thoughts* about an idea. They are the helper's opinions expressed in a particular way. They are *not* an expression of the helper's *feelings* about an idea. Because they are thoughts and tend to use evaluative terms, influencing responses must be carefully worded so as not to be personally or morally attacking. Most effective influencing responses are fairly mild or tentative in their wording, especially if negatively influencing. As such, they can be gently persuasive.

Influencing responses are a subtle form of suggestion. While some helpees are quite reluctant to take advice, they may be more susceptible to influence by the helper. Influencing responses can provide an opportunity for the helper to play "devil's advocate" and help the helpee to examine his or her ideas more carefully before deciding on any action. Or the helper can subtly prod the helpee to action through influencing because the weight of the helper's indirectly stated opinion pressures the helpee to further consider and to act on the idea. To an important degree, when a helper gives an influencing response, he or she is conveying the message "You can do it" or "You're smart enough to avoid that trap." Because this message is conveyed, the helper must be pretty certain that the helpee does have the skills at that time to carry out the encouraged idea.

Advice-Giving

Encouraging helpees to make effective decisions and to work on goals are two major aspects of assisting helpees to go forward with change. There are times when influencing responses are not effective or are not possible to use, as when the helpee does not offer ideas for the helper to influence even in response to open questions regarding alternatives. Promoting change may sometimes require advice-giving, when appropriate and necessary.

An advice-giving response presents an idea that the helper believes will aid in resolving the problem or issue. For example:

1. *Helpee:* "I think I've thought about everything possible now. I don't know what more there is."
   Helper: "I think you could also think about which alternative you've posed satisfies most of your needs now that you've identified both positive and negative consequences for all of them."
2. *Helpee:* "My roommate really gets on my nerves. She's always throwing her dirty clothes around. I've tried to set a

	good example, and sometimes I've even put her clothes away. Nothing stops her. And she doesn't take hints."
Helper:	"Telling her directly how much it bothers you is another option you have."
3. *Helpee:*	"I don't know whether to leave home and set myself up in the city or to stay home and work on the farm. I'm not sure I'm ready for such a big decision."
Helper:	"One alternative you haven't mentioned is going to the city for a specified length of time and then working on the farm for a set time to compare the two life styles."

Advice, then, originates with the *helper*. The main purpose of advice is to provide an alternative mode of behavior—either action or thoughts—that is new to the helpee.

Many helpers are reluctant to suggest to helpees what to do and therefore use advice sparingly. When a helper does give advice, it must occur at very particular times. The conditions for appropriate advice-giving are: (1) both helper and helpee quite thoroughly understand the problem(s) or issue(s), (2) the helper is aware of the alternatives that the helpee has already thought about, and (3) the helper is aware of what the helpee's reasons are for trying or rejecting those alternatives. In other words, the problem or issue must be fully explored before action toward change is considered and various options must have already been posed and examined. Most likely, such conditions will be encountered in the latter action-focused stages of the helping process, Program Planning (Stage 5) and Reviewing Action (Stage 7) in particular.

Advice-giving responses may be about thoughts ("I think you could think about . . . ") or acts ("Going for a job interview might be helpful at this point"). At times, they may be very directive, identifying what the helper believes the helpee needs to do ("You really need to go to your classes since you want to pass"). Most often, effective advice is *exploratory* ("Perhaps we could explore the factors involved in the decision first").

The effective helper is most often tentative with advice-giving. Options—not "oughts"—are suggested. Appropriate and effective advice-giving responses are presented as what the helpee *could* ponder or do, not what the helpee *should* ponder or do; what the helpee *might* consider, not what the helpee *must* consider. One helpee placed numerable shoulds and oughts on herself.

Helpee:	"I really ought to feel differently. I shouldn't feel angry at my father when he gives advice. But I hate it when he does. I end up being very bitchy and yelling at him."

Helper: "You could consider how you might change your responses to him in constructive ways."

Helpee: "I don't know what I should try that I already haven't. I've tried to ignore him. I've tried to avoid talking with him about things I know he will give me advice on. I've tried to just agree with him so he'll stop pestering me. I still get very irritated and end up being nasty or sarcastic."

Helper: "Another alternative you might experiment with is being open about your feelings. You could let him know how his advice-giving affects you."

Helpee: "Well, I *could* I suppose. That's kind of scary to me though."

Helper: "Let's look at what's scary about it and then consider how you might put it into action."

What is effective is that the helper does not impose ideas in a closed way but rather models openness of thought and action.

Whatever advice the helper does decide to suggest should be an idea which the helpee is unlikely to reach alone. Advice-giving tends to foster unwanted dependency on the helper by the helpee, characterized by the helpee looking to the helper for direction and waiting for the helper to suggest decisions and how to work through alternatives. Useful learning does not arise through such dependency. Rather, the effective helper encourages the helpee to make decisions and work through alternatives alone, with the helper's facilitation.

It is crucial that the helper have knowledge of what resources the helpee has with which to carry out any suggestions made. Resources generally refer to strengths and skills; for example, the ability to make phone calls to set up appointments, the feeling vocabulary with which to acknowledge others' feelings, sufficient confidence to set up one's own living arrangements, and so on. Resources also include pragmatic things; for example, the finances with which to pay a lawyer for consultation, the basic skills necessary to cook for oneself, or the experience requirements necessary for a particular job opening. If one or more necessary resources are lacking or are questionable, the helper must carefully consider the usefulness of posing the suggestion *at that time.* In such instances subgoals, such as learning cooking skills or rehearsing phone calls, are often necessary to consider and plan for. The same process is called for: assisting the helpee to consider and work through alternatives as much as possible alone, with the helper as guide.

If the helpee has done a great deal of the work in thinking about options but remains in need of further options or strategies, then the helper may select advice-giving as the response of choice. In doing so, presenting the suggestion tentatively as one alternative among several is preferable to voicing it as the only solution. In addition to the suggestion itself, the value of effective advice-giving is in modeling possibilities and openness to change.

When to Use Leading Responses

Leading responses—questions, influence, and advice—have generally not been viewed by many professionals as important parts of the helper's tools. The value attributed to leading responses seems to be dependent on what the helper decides are the goals of helping. If helpers see their goals as establishing effective relationships and encouraging helpees to focus on their feelings, then leading responses will not be the responses of choice. Rather, continuing responses will be most frequently used. On the other hand, leading responses can be useful if they are well thought out and planned and if the goals involve a systematic attempt to help helpees change.

The general rule is that leading responses are used *only* when a clear understanding of the situation has been achieved. They are used in conjunction with continuing responses in the Integration (Stage 4), Program Planning (Stage 5), Action-Taking (Stage 6), and Reviewing (Stage 7) Stages of the helping process (again, see Chapter 1). The reader should note that these responses are but part of the change process and that specific helping strategies (covered in Chapter 7) are necessary to promote change.

Leading responses shift the nature of the helping relationship. They are usually not considered within the core conditions that Rogers identified. In distinction from continuing responses that foster open communication, the purpose of leading responses is to facilitate helpee problem solving and problem resolution. Leading responses place some responsibility for change on the helper; that is, the helper clarifies the direction of change for the helpee and may affect it by asking questions, by subtly influencing the helpee's behavior or attitudes, or by directly giving advice about what the helpee could do. The helper does not take the responsibility for making the changes but does take responsibility for guiding the helpee to decide on and carry out any changes. The helper, in short, leads the helpee toward change.

Leading responses can be very effective. They are an important part of the helper's repertoire of behavior *when not used prematurely*. Too often helpers use leading responses before they gain the helpee's trust and confidence. Usually in these cases the helpee rejects the leads. Direction or influence from an untrusted person is seldom welcome. Another problem is that helpers sometimes use leading responses before they (and the helpees) really understand the helpees' problems or direction. This is particularly true of advice-giving. While the suggestions might be valuable, they often are not appropriate to the actual dilemma being experienced by the helpee. A solution to the wrong problem has little value.

How, then, does a helper know when to use leading responses? Before using leading responses helpers need to ask themselves:

1. Do I clearly understand the nature of the problem?
2. Do I have plans or strategies to help resolve this problem?
3. Am I willing to assume a significant part of the responsibility for guiding the helpee to focus on change and to take action?

If the helper cannot answer "yes" to all of the above, continuing responses are usually more appropriate. Most frequently, the helper will be able to respond with a confident "yes" when the helping relationship process has reached the Integration Stage. The exception to this general rule is the use of open questions, which obviously can serve a useful purpose in exploring and especially in clarifying feelings. It is the too frequent and too early use of questions that must be avoided.

SUMMARY

Since helpers' goals for helping shift not only with different helpees but also within a set of interactions with the same helpee, it is necessary for a helper to be able to employ all the different responses we've discussed. We take the position that there is no such thing as a "good" or a "bad" response. We don't agree with those who feel that helpers have no right to give advice; nor do we consider a barrage of pointed questions to be helpful. Rather, we feel helpers' words must be appropriate to their context and purpose. We don't feel as though a good standard recipe for helping exists that says, for example, mixing 20% of content and 40% of affective responses with varying portions of other responses will be effective. On the other hand, the helper's main ingredients—the words—must be of high quality and they must be mixed in proper proportions to attain the specific goals of each particular helping relationship. In general, most helpers will find that the majority of their responses will be continuing responses. Variations in balance between leading and continuing responses will occur as the relationship progresses to consider specific change goals and strategies for change. In addition, a third major category of responses, self-referent responses, are available for use by a helper and must also be considered in terms of helping goals. Self-referent responses are discussed in the following chapter.

THOUGHT QUESTIONS

1. What do continuing responses accomplish?
2. Why can premature leading responses be so problematic?
3. Can people learn to be empathic? How?
4. Why are affective responses so important?
5. How often do you try to influence your friends or give them advice?
6. Which of the responses discussed in this chapter do you use frequently in your conversations?
7. How does the helper change the helping relationship by using leading responses?
8. Which response would you expect to be the most difficult for you to use?
9. How does influence differ from advice?
10. Give several examples of choices of words that helpers could make that would increase their helpees' defensiveness.

5

The Words of Helping: II. Self-Referent Responses

A marriage counselor, just recently divorced, listens intently to his client's marital problems. Some of the conflicts and worries sound familiar to him; in fact, he had the very same feelings just before he asked his wife for a divorce. Yes, he knows what it's like to try to separate from someone so important.

A welfare caseworker is listening to a wife's story of how her husband abuses her and her children. It seems incredible to the worker that a woman could be so willing to continue suffering. The caseworker thinks, "If that were me, I'd get him arrested right away."

A counselor working with veterans has heard one war story too many. His own experiences in a POW camp make most of his clients' experiences pale by comparison. When a man comes to him and relates the story of his war wound with anguish and tears, the counselor says "Grow up, buddy. If you think you have it bad, let me tell you what happened to me...."

Feelings of annoyance and irritation are becoming more apparent to a psychologist working with disadvantaged girls. The frustration in trying to help one particular girl never ends. She refuses to try anything the psychologist suggests, she complains about everything, and, to top it off, she's verbally abusive. Feeling herself near to exploding, the psychologist asks herself, "Should I tell her how I feel? Should I let her know what's going on inside me?"

This chapter will explore the question the last helper has asked herself. In all of these examples, the helper had personal information to share. The information was either a *personal experience* or a *personal reaction to the helpee*. Some of the helpers hesitated to let the helpee know what they were feeling; the veterans' counselor was the exception.

The question "What should I let the helpee know about me?" is an important one for a helper to consider. It can mean the difference between the helper being seen as a caring, genuine, *sharing* person or a distant, impersonal on-looker. As discussed in Chapter 4, genuineness is one of the core conditions for helping. But how does a helper convey genuineness? The helper can answer this question by saying "I'll tell the helpee whatever he or she wants to know about me." The helper also has the option of saying "My life is my business. Why should I tell this person anything about me, except insofar as my helping experience is concerned?" Finally, the helper can carefully consider how to talk about personal concerns, answering the question—for the moment—in this way: "It depends."

What such sharing depends on is precisely what is under consideration in this chapter. The helper's *use of self* is inherently different from the verbal responses covered in the last chapter. The reasons are simple. For one, the helper is *sharing* something about himself or herself. The helpee then learns more about the helper as a person—the helper's emotions, background, even difficulties. What should the helper share? What should the helper keep private? Why should the helper disclose at all? Secondly, the helper is taking a *risk*, a chance to let the helpee in on her or his world. It is a chance that can either enhance or detract from the helping relationship. Lastly, in using personal experiences as helping responses, the *helper* becomes the focus of the relationship, if only briefly. The helper is saying "Wait a second. I've got something to share." The roles are reversed. The helpee becomes listener, the helper speaker. *How can the helper use this reversal to help the helpee?* This is the key criterion.

TWO DEFINITIONS

Since helpers' use of self is such a broad concept, we've found it useful to make further distinctions. We term any verbal response which concerns the helper himself or herself a *self-referent* response. There are two types of self-referent responses: *self-disclosure* and *self-involving*. These concern different uses of the helper's experiences. Consider these two exchanges.

1. *Helpee:* "I find myself furious with my boss. No matter what I do, he finds fault. He never says anything good about my work, and I put in so many extra hours."

    Helper: "I've had a similar experience working here. I found it really helpful to tell my supervisor how I felt. She was really understanding."

2. *Helpee:* "I've tried to find work, really I have. What can I do if they feel I'm not young enough? I'm over 50 and they want a 20-year-old."

Helper: "Tom, I'm surprised to hear you talking that way. I'm really confident that you'll find a job if you keep trying. You can't give up so easily."

The first example is *self-disclosure,* the second, *self-involving.* Both involve the helper telling the helpee something personal. They differ in terms of *what* the helper talks about. In self-disclosing, the helper discusses personal *experiences.* In self-involving, the helper discloses personal *reactions* to something the helpee has said. (confrontation)

Self-disclosing can involve recent or past events in the helper's life. It can be anything from "I spent a weekend in Philadelphia once" to "My husband and I are having serious problems, too." But it tells *about the helper.* In a sense, it's a story (usually short) about the helper that is given in response to something the helpee is experiencing. *Self-involving* is usually more immediate, more direct. The helper verbally reacts to what the helpee has said or done. While self-disclosure is *personal,* self-involving is *interpersonal;* that is, the helper discusses a thought or feeling about the *helpee.* The resulting impact is that the helping relationship is brought to the fore very directly as a helping tool.

The helper is being honest and open—that is, genuine—in using these types of responses. In self-disclosure, the focus of the response is on the helper; in self-involving, the focus of the helper's personal response is on the helpee. In both cases, the helper is talking personally and sharing something, whether relevant experiences or feelings, with the helpee.

WHY TALK ABOUT ONESELF?

One viewpoint about helper self-disclosure and self-involving is that they have no place in helping, that the helper should keep experiences and feelings private. According to this perspective, the helper is there to listen, not to discuss personal problems or reactions. And indeed, helping *is* different from friendship, different from casual conversation where two people freely exchange personal information. As we will see shortly, there are effective and ineffective ways of using self-referent responses. But before discussing these, what about the more basic question: what purpose do these responses serve?

As we suggest in other chapters, the helper's use of *any* response is for one reason: *the helpee's benefit.* The basic criterion for saying or doing anything in helping is not how "turned on" the helper feels or how satisfied or content with a certain response. Nor is the criterion how the helpee *feels.* Simply stated, the criterion is this: *does what the helper says encourage the helpee to explore himself or herself? Does it facilitate helpee growth and development?* It is from this perspective that self-referent responses must be considered. Think about the following brief interactions in this light.

1. *Helpee:* "I've been having the toughest time with my mother. I love her, but I find it nearly impossible to talk with her."
   Helper 1: "I have trouble talking with my mother, too. She was just with me for several days and a lot of the old conflicts just interfered. I get discouraged."
   Helpee: "What do you do when that happens?"
2. *Helpee:* "I've been having the toughest time with my mother. I love her, but I find it nearly impossible to talk with her."
   Helper 2: "I've found it difficult at times to talk with my mother. What I've found helpful is to observe how other people respond to her at those or similar times. What I see is that there are different responses than I ordinarily make. I wonder how *you* respond at those difficult times."
   Helpee: "I never thought of seeing how other people react. I bet that would be interesting. My own responses get stilted. I find myself getting irritated and responding in a clipped way. Or I start to withdraw and not really listen. I don't like myself when I do either. I think I'll try to watch how other people respond."

Both helpers were self-disclosing, but which seemed more helpful? What Helper 1 said apparently removed the focus from the helpee to the helper, with the resulting effect that the helpee maintained the role switch and urged the helper to talk on. What Helper 2 said briefly shifted roles but quickly righted them. The resulting effect was that the helpee looked at his *own* behavior, though in the context of the helper's disclosure. The helper's self-disclosure in the second instance gave impetus to helpee exploration.

What, then, are the general effects of effective self-referent responses on the helpee? The two basic effects of such responses are: (1) the personal involvement effect and (2) the modeling effect.

Personal Involvement

As we've earlier emphasized, helpers are human, too. Imagine an interaction in which one person talks endlessly about himself or herself while the other merely listens. How would the speaker react to this silent mirror? Probably by beginning to wonder about this person, beginning to imagine about his or her life, and perhaps by even getting angry at the other for being so closed. The other person becomes less real, less personal, more an object. Take the example one step closer to helping: imagine that the speaker has a serious personal problem. If the listener never discusses anything personal, the speaker would most likely begin to be more guarded—"Maybe this person thinks I'm crazy. Maybe she's never had this problem or any problem. I bet she doesn't understand." A helper who does not use any self-referent talk does not allow the helpee to see her or him as another human being.

By using self-disclosure or self-involving, the helper takes a fairly important step. The helper reveals *humanness*—feelings and experiences, weaknesses and problems, as well as strengths and resources. On an unspoken level, the communication is, "Look, I'm a real person, too. And I'm willing to let you into my life some." But it's a risk, for the same reason the helpee is reluctant to disclose. Specifically, the helper becomes vulnerable, open to possible rejection, possibly to being looked down upon. This is the central risk of any close relationship, after all. Most people would love to have many close friends with whom they can share their experiences, but the fear of nonacceptance is a strong inhibitor. By taking the risk the helper becomes "personally involved," and the helpee begins to know the helper *as a person*. The helper no longer plays the role of an objective, distant listener. It is a vital message that the helper gives to the helpee: "I am asking you to trust me; I will trust you also." Then the helper becomes less mysterious, less perfect, more real. The helpee is more likely to continue, since it is difficult to be defensive and closed with someone who shares. Anecdotal data include statements like "I didn't mean to be so revealing. But when he was so open, I felt like I should be, too." Partners shed defensiveness when the other person is personally sharing.

Because of this, self-disclosure and self-involving promote the helpee's being freer with the helper. In other words, optimal helper self-reference facilitates helpee personal involvement in the helping interaction. An interesting example involved a new helpee, an adolescent girl who was quite perturbed about being in a counseling situation. While she was cooperative, she remained guarded even in the third session. It was not until the helpee mentioned an avid interest in stereo equipment that the helping interaction became less stilted. The helpee spoke more freely, her eyes lit up, and she seemed enthused for the first time. The helper quickly seized the opportunity to promote greater involvement by using a salient self-referent response: "I've got a poor receiver, too, which my wife and I have wanted to replace for years. The power seems insufficient to produce the sound we'd like. You say you're considering a receiver *and* an amplifier. I'm interested in how you've come to that decision." This captured the helpee's interest, and she readily picked up on the opening. The helpee became more relaxed and more willing to talk about other matters, a common reaction among children and teenagers especially. Entry (Stage 1) was, therefore, facilitated by helper self-reference.

Think about it this way. In meeting others for the first time, we tend to be guarded. We don't always know what or how much to say. A self-protective mechanism operates in such a situation. What we are really doing is assuring ourselves that a particular relationship will be beneficial and satisfying before we begin to reveal ourselves. Our interpersonal "radar" operates, scanning the social world for signals to begin the acquaintanceship process. A self-disclosure from the helper may provide the helpee with the signal needed for her or him to feel freer to open up.

For example, one of the authors was involved with a new helpee who was clearly feeling self-conscious about the problem which led him to seek help.

Helpee: "I'm embarrassed. You must think I'm crazy. I think I'm crazy! Really, I ought to be able to cope with this myself. Moving to a new place shouldn't be so traumatic. Then why am I here?"

Helper: "You're feeling quite foolish for not being able to quickly make the changes."

Helpee: "Yes, I am. After all, my complaints about the place seem foolish even to me. But I can't seem to help it."

Helper: "You've found it difficult to shift between life in a big city and life in a smaller community. I did too, initially. Coming from the New York area to here was a major change for me. And things like shopping, restaurants, choices in movies—the things you've felt let down about—I felt down about, too, for a while. I grew to really enjoy living here, though. Right now, it's difficult for you to imagine enjoying it."

Helpee: "You mean you felt the same way I do? That sure is helpful to hear. I really felt like a fool for being homesick for my old town, and for such material things, too! I kept thinking I was being childish, immature, you know. You mean other people go through the same kinds of feelings, so I don't have to feel so dumb...."

It seems clear that a brief self-disclosure by the helper was an important signal for this helpee. He was very taken by the helper's revelation and seemed relieved. His relief allowed him, as you have seen, to talk more personally about his feelings—awkward feelings that are hard to reveal to a stranger. This helpee became more personally involved as a function of an appropriate self-referent response, in this case a self-disclosure.

Modeling

Research on self-disclosure (see Suggested Readings) suggests that a reciprocity effect occurs after one person talks about personal matters to another. The discloser is modeling, or demonstrating, how he or she would like the interaction to proceed. This has also been termed the "dyadic effect" in that the two people begin to form a "rule" about their level of openness. Interestingly enough, individuals who do not ordinarily tell others much about themselves will increase their disclosure after talking to someone who discloses personal information. Given these findings, helpers can provide their helpees with good examples of openness and honesty by sharing their experiences and feelings. Furthermore, since helpers would assumedly use *effective* self-referent responses, the helpee would learn how to discuss personal issues with others without becoming overbearing, a concern many people have in revealing themselves.

Consider this example in which the helper's self-involving responses were given one session earlier than the helpee's more personal response:

Session A
  Helper: "You've been worried that you *can't* change. I've been feeling frustrated because I don't seem to know yet how to help you to change."
  Helpee: "Mmm.... I don't know what'll help me. It's a pattern I've seen all my life. To start something but never follow through."
  Helper: "Not completing any one change frustrates you. I worry that you allow your frustration to block any further movement. You've begun several important steps toward change recently. But a hitch in one seems to get you so low that you stop working in the other areas."
  Helpee: "I know I just feel like giving up. Feel like, what's the use?"
  Helper: "You get pretty upset with yourself when your progress doesn't go smoothly."
  Helpee: "Yes, I feel terribly disappointed. And wonder if I should bother."
  Helper: "Sometimes making changes seems futile to you. It makes me sad to hear you talk like this now. I hoped you were less caught up in that sense of hopelessness and I was very pleased to see you start in on some concrete changes...."

Session B
  Helpee: "I was upset last time when I left."

Helper: "I'd like to hear what upset you."
Helpee: "I felt you were mad at me. And irritated."
Helper: "You worried that I was annoyed with you."
Helpee: "Yeah, I was very worried that you were so annoyed that you wouldn't want to see me anymore."
Helper: "You were afraid that I would end our relationship. I'm confused about what made you feel that way."
Helpee: "When you were talking about being frustrated with me about the changes, I got the sense that you were very unhappy with me. And so I thought you might want to call it quits."
Helper: "Because I shared my worry with you, you feared I was leading to terminating the relationship. Let me share more of my feelings with you now. I don't recall feeling irritated, but rather perplexed; how can I best assist you in making these changes that are so difficult for you? I certainly do feel frustrated—much of that frustration is for myself, that I haven't yet been fully able to be of the best help that I'd like to be. But some of that frustration is indeed for you, for your behavior. I found myself getting a bit impatient with your tendency to completely give up on all levels when confronted with one problem in one area. I've felt very excited by the changes you have made, and I'm most hopeful about the changes you can continue to make. But I believe we have to focus on your habit of giving up all when one problem occurs in a limited area."
Helpee: "So even though you feel frustrated, it's not all for me. And you're saying we need to go on, so you don't want to end things. That's a relief. I guess I went too far, but I always expect to be dumped when someone gets annoyed at me. And I'm afraid to say anything."
Helper: "I'm *very* pleased you felt free to tell me you were upset with what I said last time. I think that's a significant step forward, a real change. Your willingness to do so has made me feel closer to you, and that's important...."

The modeling effect leads to the creation of a certain kind of relationship. We tend to disclose to those we like and like those to whom we reveal ourselves. A relationship may therefore be formed in which a helper's self-reference leads the helpee to feel esteemed or valued. Although it would not be helpful if the discussions were completely reciprocal so the helper was expected to match any helpee intimacy, a well-planned helper self-disclosure or self-involving response may serve to increase the intimacy level of the interaction considerably.

These two general purposes of self-referent responses—personal involvement and modeling—serve several common goals. They let the helpee know that the helper is a person with a past, a present, and a future, with thoughts, feelings, and goals. They demonstrate how one can honestly express oneself in a close interaction. They further the creation of an atmosphere in which the helpee feels valued and important. They lead the helpee to take risks, to see that honesty does not have to lead to rejection.

AUTHENTICITY OR SELFISHNESS?

Despite these advantages of self-referent responses, they are difficult responses for helpers to use well. This is due partly to lack of skill but is also related to attitudes regarding talking about oneself in a helping relationship. Two opposite attitudes are found in helpers: (1) that self-referent responses must be absolutely authentic and (2) that self-referent responses are selfish. Each of these attitudes has a kernel of truth to it. Let's examine each.

The "Real Helper." From the first point of view, helpers must be "real," "authentic," or "up-front" when talking about themselves. This seems fairly obvious: how could anyone disagree? But *how* "real" should a helper be?

Let's go back to the veterans' counselor. His "If you think *you* have it bad . . . " response was real. He felt it sincerely and in that sense was being up-front with the helpee. Let's also assume, for the sake of argument, that a particular helper simply does not like a certain helpee. Authenticity would suggest that the helper divulge this dislike. But in either of these situations *is the helper being helpful?* The extreme point of view suggests that *whatever* feeling or reaction a helper has must be "shared" with the helpee and will be helpful because it is authentic. To do otherwise is viewed as deceptive. Certain approaches to helping stress the *absolute genuineness of the relationship* as the medium of change. Modeling and the experience of a genuine relationship counter the destructive relationships in the helpee's life. Unfortunately, such an extreme use of self-referent responses tends to make the helpee's reaction secondary; that is, it places too great an emphasis on the helper's experiences during the interaction and tends to shift the roles of speaker and listener too frequently and/or too permanently.

Listen to the following exchange.

Helper: "I've been sitting here thinking what a pleasant person you are. I like you."

94   CHAPTER 5

Helpee: "Oh, thanks. Gee, I don't know what to say."
Helper: "As I see it, that's one of your troubles. You fail to respond to what others say to you in a way that keeps interest up."
Helpee: "Well, I am not sure how to respond. Maybe you have ideas."
Helper: "I'm not sure I have ideas, but I can share with you my reactions to you."
Helpee: "Okay."
Helper: "We've met several times. As I said, I find you a very pleasant person. I have also felt somewhat bored while you've been talking. Maybe you've noticed me yawning from time to time?"
Helpee: "Yes, I have. I thought you were tired."
Helper: "No, I was restless. I was getting impatient with you."
Helpee: "I'm awfully sorry."
Helper: "No need for you to be sorry. What I'm telling you is that there is something about your style that made me bored and soon impatient. I didn't feel like I could listen much longer."
Helpee: "I *have* noticed that you talk a lot . . . ."

What did you notice about this interaction? Was the helper being real? How did the helper demonstrate genuineness? What was the helpee's response? What might the helpee have derived from this "real" helper's responses? In what ways might the helper's genuineness have hindered the helping relationship? How might the helping goals have been differently approached?

The "Selfish" Helper. On the other hand, openness and honesty by helpers are viewed by some as solely selfish. From this point of view, talking about oneself can hardly help another person, particularly one who is coming to you for advice. From this perspective, a helper who discusses himself or herself is meeting personal needs irrelevant to the helpee and is using the helping relationship for personal reasons. This position, taken to *its* extreme, would dictate no self-referent responses. Yet, we have seen in earlier discussions of helpers' needs (see Chapter 2) that some personal needs are not only met in helping but are the impetus for helping. In other words, helpers are to some extent "selfish" in their helping. The question arises again: how do these responses help? If they cannot be seen as helping the other person, they should be avoided.

Consider the following interaction.

Helpee: "I can't help but wonder how you feel about what I've just said."

Helper:	"You're curious about my reaction."
Helpee:	"Yes. I'd like to know what you think."
Helper:	"What I think is important to you."
Helpee:	"Of course it is. I wouldn't be coming here to see you otherwise."
Helper:	"If my opinion weren't valuable, you'd not be here."
Helpee:	"That's what I've said, yes. So I'd like to know."
Helper:	"You're feeling irritated because I haven't given you the response you'd like."
Helpee:	"Yes, I suppose that's true. I do feel annoyed that you haven't said anything yet."
Helper:	"When others don't respond to you as you wish, you get annoyed."
Helpee:	"Yes, I guess that's true. I do like people to respond directly and I feel very put off when they don't . . . ."

What did you notice about this interaction? Was the helper being selfish? If so, how? If not, why not? Was the helper being real? If so, how? If not, how not? What was the helpee's response? What might the helpee have derived from the helper's "unselfish" responses? In what ways may the helper's "unselfish" responses have hindered the helping relationship? How might the helping goals have been differently approached?

To Use or Not to Use

The insistence that there can be a rule about the helper's using self-referent responses leads to obvious problems. As suggested in the examples above, honesty *can* be real but cruel, and it can be used in selfish ways. But it is also true that too *little* personal exposure can hurt a helping relationship. Indeed, avoiding personal exposure may itself be selfish.

The extreme positions do not answer the question: *what types of self-referent responses are effective at what points in helping?* Self-referent responses must be used well by a helper. We will now discuss how to use oneself effectively for both self-disclosure and self-involving and how to avoid poor self-referent responses.

Self-Disclosure

Self-disclosure can be thought of in terms of three dimensions: *type, intensity,* and *duration.* There are two general *types* of self-disclosure—biographical and personal. Biographical self-disclosure concerns one's history and present circumstances.

1. "I am a clinical psychologist by training. I received my Ph.D. from the University of Connecticut."
2. "I used to live on Long Island, not very far from Manhattan. So I am familiar with the area you're talking about."
3. "Right now I spend some time teaching and doing research at the University as well as seeing clients."

It is relatively easy to discuss these facts since they are generally not very personal. Personal self-disclosure concerns one's more private self: thoughts and feelings, plans and goals, strengths and weaknesses, cares and concerns.

1. "Frankly, I am uncertain of how to arrange my schedule once the baby is born. I've done a lot of thinking about it, but haven't yet been able to identify an effective plan. I think I need to see how this baby nurses and work from the basis of that schedule. Within a couple of weeks, it'll be clear and I'll begin scheduling again."
2. "My own goals in relationships include enriched openness and caring and greater mutuality. Intimacy is vital to me."
3. "I believe that one of my own strengths, for example, is that I attempt to anticipate and plan for things to come."

Personal self-disclosure is more difficult to discuss than biographical since it is more intimate. It reveals some of the inner person of the helper to the helpee.

Personal disclosure can occur with varying degrees of *intensity*. One can discuss one's personal goals in a very intense, honest way or in a superficial, uninvolved way.

More Intense Disclosures

1. "I want my own relationships to be genuine. I know I need to strive for greater directness; it means so much to me that I always feel warmed when others are real with me."
2. "I have some trouble planning ahead myself. I'm not certain what the problem is, but I think I don't spend sufficient time thinking through what I will need or want for certain tasks. I get disturbed with myself for that."
3. "What I believe is that we are helped by seeking out *patterns*

More Uninvolved Disclosures

1. "I want my relationships to be genuine. I believe genuineness is so critical to relationships."

2. "I have some trouble planning ahead myself. I suppose all of us do at one time or another."

3. "What I believe is that we are helped by seeking out *patterns*

| of behavior. It's these patterns, habits of interaction and reaction, which can be destructive or problematic. I think we all can benefit from identifying aspects we can change, to reach important personal goals we each have. I try to do so myself, for sure." | of behavior. You need to make changes in them, for your own good." |

Finally, disclosure can last for a short or long duration of time. A helper could dominate the relationship by spending half of an interview discussing himself or herself. Or the helper could moderate her or his disclosures to last for short spans so as not to dominate the interaction.

Lengthy Duration
1. "I have had similar experiences with weight. Over the years, I put weight on, took it off, put it on, took it off, and so on. I think my weight loss would be maintained as long as I was happy with my work—and/or the relationship I was in. On the other hand, once I was very content in a relationship, I'd start eating again, for fun. So it wasn't just the one aspect—being unhappy. I'd eat when I was happy, too. I've been discouraged, as you have. And I have wondered about the likelihood of ever keeping off the weight more permanently, as you are. But I have been determined to do so. I found an eating program which made sense to me. It has not only a recommended eating plan, but fine recipes, too. These I have found helpful in maintaining interest and in keeping one satisfied. Of course, I end up putting more effort in it. And the time it takes sometimes bothers me. But I've been able to relearn eating habits that are more balanced in terms of nutrition and quantity. That I appreciate. I find I feel better, as I expect you will if you choose to use it."

Moderate Duration
2. "I have sometimes felt keenly pulled toward a different career. Having been interested in films since I was very young, I have nurtured this interest. At times, I have seriously considered how I might combine my interests, and I have indeed been able to do so to an as yet limited extent, as I believe you are thinking of doing."

Brief Duration
3. "My own family life I find incredibly hectic—and intensely satisfying. At times, like you, I believe the very complexity of our lives adds to the enjoyment."

Obviously, these are limited examples of the variations in duration that helpers use. So far, though, there has been no mention of the effects of disclosure on the helpee nor the appropriateness of any of the examples given.

These factors—type, intensity, and duration—are critical in determining the appropriateness or effectiveness of the helper's disclosure. This is because they can tip the balance between a helpful and a selfish self-disclosure.

Guidelines

Type of disclosure can have a strong impact on the helpee. Biographical disclosure is primarily useful for simple conversational purposes—that is, sharing information to keep the interaction interesting. It is seldom helpful in the sense that it aids the helpee in resolving a pressing concern. While it does encourage closeness, it is a closeness based on impersonal dimensions. It can, of course, start a relationship and to this degree can be important. It also is relevant when responding to queries by helpees regarding background, training, and experience. Often helpees seek such biographical information in the Entry Stage (Stage 1) or occasionally in the Exploration Stage (Stage 2). However, too much focus on this type of disclosure may turn the helping relationship into a conversation and thereby stall help. Therefore, helpers generally should avoid biographical disclosures and, when appropriate to use, should keep them brief and to the point.

Personal self-disclosure is a different matter. By revealing something ordinarily not discussed, the helper shows the helpee a willingness to step forward and be known. But how can this be done in a helpful way? There are two basic questions to answer: (1) *What is my goal in using this response?* and (2) *What response am I likely to get in return?* The following guidelines should help in considering these questions.

The first guideline is to consider what you will disclose. Not everything about yourself that is related to the helpee should be brought up. Just because you do share a concern or a problem does not mean you should say so. *You must consider how your own personal experience can benefit the helpee.* It is not enough to say that the helpee will then know that the helper is "human," that others have similar worries. Let's assume that you *have not* resolved your problem—it's still bothering you a lot. Will sharing this help? Let's assume you *have* resolved your problem. Will sharing your particular set of circumstances, ideas, and solutions help? Do they apply to this particular helpee's situation and opportunities for development and change?

Compare these two examples of disclosure.

> *Helpee:* "I'd love to go back to work. But with my three kids, I feel really guilty, especially if no one's home to see them after school. I think I'll put it off for a few years."

Helper 1: "After my last child, I insisted that we hire a babysitter right away. I felt really good about that."

Helper 2: "I feel the same way about my kids. But I worked out a way to get back to work since I knew I'd be unhappy if I didn't."

Both helpers are being "authentic." These are sincere and honest statements. Yet the first helper's response may lead the helpee to feel inadequate. "After all," the helper is really saying, "if I can do it, why can't you?" The second helper's disclosure, equally honest, is more appropriate and more effective because it is likely to enable the helpee to think again about her decision. It may encourage further exploration, not discourage it. This, then, is the second guideline: *Disclose aspects of yourself that will encourage the helpee to seek additional ways of working at the concern.* Do not disclose personal situations that seem futile, hopeless, or impossible to change since this may not be true of the helpee's situation. Often, this type of disclosure is helpful during the Integration (Stage 4), Program Planning (Stage 5), and Action-Taking (Stage 6) Stages.

The last guideline concerns the duration of self-disclosure: *keep it short.* Self-disclosing responses should be facilitative to the helpee. A lengthy, detailed focus on the helper's experiences can focus the helpee on the helper. Conversation shifts the emphasis to the one doing the most talking, and the helpee begins to pay more attention to the helper's situation than to her or his own. A short, relevant personal experience of the helper can help the helpee think, can facilitate the helpee's considering other ways of doing things, and can promote the helpee's realization that problems can be solved. But if the helper's disclosure is extensive, especially if it suggests that life-situations are basically unresolvable, then the helper has become helpee and vice versa. Consider these two possible responses to the helpee's statement. Which of the two helper responses is the more effective disclosure?

Helpee: "I have such problems talking with my parents. They always treat me like their little boy, even though I'm 30 now."

Helper 1: "My parents were the same way. My father always wanted me to go into his business—he's a successful businessman in town. He's convinced I don't know how to run my life. In fact, he even tried to buy a house for me a few years ago. He thought I'd get cheated, so why shouldn't he do it? Thank God my mother's not as crazy as he is!"

Helper 2: "That can be really tough. I'm in a similar position with my parents. I really get furious when they do that."

SELF-INVOLVING

Like self-disclosure, self-involving responses also vary in intensity and duration. Unlike self-disclosure, self-involving responses are more directly given to the helpee *about the helpee*. The helper's thoughts, feelings, and reactions about what the helpee has said or done are discussed.

1. "I am very pleased that you decided to go to the assertiveness group. It is encouraging to me to see you willing to take the risk."
2. "I want to let you know how your responses have affected me. I feel closed off from you when you respond so defensively, as in your last statement. I'm concerned that you continue to jump on what I say, as if you need to defend yourself."
3. "When you told me just now that my remark had pained you, I felt really close to you. I appreciate your letting me know so we can talk about it openly."

Often such responses have been termed *confrontation*, although this term suggests that they are argumentative in nature. Good self-involving, in fact, should be anything but argumentative. The helper's goal is not to attack the helpee. Rather, as Egan (1976) notes, the goal is to invite the helpee "to examine his [or her] behavior and its consequences more carefully" (p. 173). In this sense, self-involving responses are confrontational in nature. They invite the helpee to confront himself or herself.

Attacking

1. "I find your behavior most annoying when you insist on arguing with me. It's immature."

2. "Your being so closed to change really stumps me. I get angry when you are never willing to try anything different."

3. "I'm terribly upset that you decided to take that job without looking into other ones as well. I feel like we've wasted our time."

Invitational

1. "I find your behavior most annoying when you argue with each statement I make. It distresses me and I find myself feeling less like talking with you."

2. "When you refuse to consider a change, as you just did, I feel stumped."

3. "I'm very glad that you decided to take action. I feel somewhat disappointed, though, that you did not look into the other possibilities in order to have the information available, as we discussed, and make the most personally satisfying decision."

Self-involving statements that have the effect of attacking the helpee are often hidden name-calling responses or shaming responses. As in the examples above, these sorts of statements tend to be absolutistic in content and to be discouraging in tone. They elicit defensive responses from the helpee rather than self-exploratory responses. The invitational self-involving responses are more specific. They do not shame or ridicule the helpee but rather convey how the helpee's behavior has affected the helper in an immediate sense. Therefore, they invite the helpee to also look at how her or his behavior has that impact. They open the door to self-examination, often in the context of interpersonal impact. Guidelines for appropriate stage usage are difficult to formulate, but perhaps self-involving responses are most frequently helpful in the Clarification (Stage 3), Program Planning (Stage 5), Action-Taking (Stage 6), Reviewing (Stage 7), and Termination (Stage 8) Stages.

The same general guideline for self-disclosure duration holds for self-involving: keep it short. But the issues regarding intensity are somewhat different. The purpose of self-involving is for the helper *to provide immediate personal reactions to the helpee*. These may be positive or negative, but they should be *present-oriented* and *personal*. Mild or moderate intensity is appropriate. Consider these two exchanges.

Helpee: "I tried not to drink. Really I did. I went into the bar just to talk with my buddies. I ordered a coke. But somehow, by the time I left, I had had several beers. Someone must've bought them for me."

Helper 1: "Joe, I really get annoyed with you. You can't do anything right. I've tried so hard, week after week, to get you off booze. You're really a fool and I feel like you're a liar as well."

Helper 2: "Joe, I'm really disappointed in you. You've done a good job so far; I really wish you could've avoided that place. Sometimes I really wonder if you really care about your physical condition."

Self-involving can be too intense and threatening. Although the first helper's *feelings* may be valid, he or she did not have to report these very intense feelings without thinking through their implications. Again, responses that make the helpee more defensive are not usually effective. On the other hand, the helper should share honest feelings with the helpee. The second helper did so, with moderate self-involving statements. How can this dilemma—just what makes for effective *and* appropriate self-involving—be resolved?

The following guidelines will make self-involving more effective.

1. Own personal feelings:
   a. "*I* feel hurt...."

102   CHAPTER 5

   b. "*I* am excited . . . ."
   c. "*I* feel encouraged . . . ."
2. Talk about present feelings:
   a. "I *feel* hurt" vs. "I *felt* hurt."
   b. "I *am* excited" vs. "I *was* excited."
   c. "I *feel* encouraged" vs. "I *felt* encouraged."
3. Explain the behaviors that lead to the feelings:
   a. "I feel hurt *because you lied to me about* . . . ."
   b. "I am excited *that you made the application to graduate school.*"
   c. "I feel encouraged *by your being able to control your angry responses* in that situation."
4. Avoid moralistic put-downs:
   a. "I can't believe you'd say that."
   b. "Only a fool would take drugs again."
   c. "One shouldn't sacrifice one's own needs for someone else's is what I believe."

SUMMARY

By following the suggestions for self-referent responses, the helper can use them judiciously. The dangers of being overbearing, of dominating the conversation and becoming helpee, or of threatening the helpee, can be avoided by thinking carefully about the self-referent responses you intend to use. By using them appropriately, the helper can be appropriately "authentic" and "selfish" at the same time. In other words, the helper can disclose experiences and feelings in an honest way and relax and be more open in the relationship. But even those responses are to be guided by the basic rule of helping: be sure that what you say and do is helpful for the helpee and not only for the helper.

THOUGHT QUESTIONS

1. How comfortable would you be in discussing your own life with your helpees?
2. How comfortable would you be in sharing your feelings about a helpee with him or her?
3. How would you feel if a helpee asked you about your sex life?
4. What are the disadvantages of being authentic and spontaneous?
5. What are the functions served by self-referent responses?
6. How can self-referent responses be selfish?
7. How do self-referent responses differ from continuing responses? from leading responses?
8. Which of the two self-referent responses would be harder for you to make? Why?
9. Give an example of an ineffective and an effective self-disclosure.
10. Give an example of an ineffective and an effective self-involving response.

6
Understanding Others' Communications

Understanding others is a basic goal of helping. Although some might suggest that *changing* helpees is a more important goal, *understanding* precedes change. Indeed, a helper focusing excessively on change, on resolving problems, may actually "solve" the wrong problem. A helper preoccupied with *doing* something useful is likely to leave little time or attention to listening and to understanding. Helping others change is a *narrowing* process. Planning of change strategies, whether in a classroom, a counseling session, or a hospital ward, demands careful consideration of the helpee's options and capabilities for change. It requires the helper to narrow down, with the helpee, exactly what is to be changed and what specific steps to take. Understanding, on the other hand, begins at least as a *broadening* process. Effective understanding occurs only when helpers allow their eyes and minds to be wide open. Understanding is a hypothesis-generating process that can easily become thwarted by a perspective too confined to the helpee's concerns. The helpee's stated problem *may* or *may not* be the underlying problem.

The tentative nature of understanding is all-important. The helper acts like a scientist tackling the explanation of a particular phenomenon. In doing research, a phenomenon is carefully observed to be sure that it exists. The observations contribute to understanding "what" it is. A broad view is then taken, as the researcher proceeds to generate *several* ideas or hypotheses to explain "why" the phenomenon occurs. Finally, the research is carried out to gather evidence that will confirm or refute the hypotheses. The explanation most consistent with the facts is considered proven. However, in research, as in helping, nothing is ever really proven beyond a doubt. More often, some hypotheses are considered more valid than others, based upon the current evidence *and* the current interpretations of that evidence.

In like manner, the helper proceeds in attempting to understand others. First, the helper must *observe*. Second, the helper must *generate several guesses* or *hypotheses* about the helpee's situation. Finally, the helper must attempt to support these hypotheses using additional information. Some helpers consider the accuracy of their predicting the helpee's future behavior to demonstrate their understanding, much as researchers rely on predictive accuracy to verify their hypotheses.

Just like scientists, helpers must always remember the tentative nature of their understanding. It is difficult in helping situations to gather "facts" about helpees' problems and concerns. More often, the helper relies upon a "reading" of others' reports of the helpee's situation. The helpee, of course, has a personal perspective on the concern and this must be genuinely respected. However, this must also be placed in context as another source of data. Taking data from these various sources and constructing a reasonable, but tentative, hypothesis is the crux of the process of understanding. Yet the process does not stop there. Indeed, it never ceases since people's lives are always changing. The helper is likewise always trying to understand a changing phenomenon—the helpee's life. Understanding others comes from careful quiet observation. A helper can never understand a helpee in a definitive way. Rather, the helper can have a grasp on the helpee's situation at a certain point in time.

Understanding, as we've presented it, may seem so broad as to be overwhelming. How can the helper know what to look at? What is involved in understanding? Actually, the process of developing understanding *is* an incredible task. It is also rather presumptuous: most of us don't really understand our own behavior, much less that of others. Furthermore, understanding can be based on various perspectives.

Take as an example a child-abusing father being seen by a family court counselor. How can his abuse of his child be *understood*? One might immediately say, "I simply *can't* understand child abuse. How could any adult kick a 5-year-old child?" This is an understanding (or lack of understanding) based on *moral issues.* The behavior is understood as "immoral," as contrary to accepted standards of parent/child relationships. However, perhaps the community in which these parents reside is more tolerant of aggressive methods for problem resolution. This behavior, then, may be an extreme example of a *subcultural norm.* Still, it is extreme. Most parents do not kick and beat their children in this neighborhood, so other reasons for his specific behavior pattern are needed. Perhaps an *economic* understanding is possible. Is the family so destitute that they are desperate and frustrated? Is the father, the traditional "breadwinner," responding to this pressure in a violent way? Obviously it is not only economic since not every poor parent responds in such a way. There are, therefore, *psychological* reasons, too—issues related to the unique personality of this father and to the unique constellation of family life of which he is a part. All of these perspectives, furthermore, are from an observer. What is the father's own understanding of his outbursts? How does the mother, a participant and an observer, view the situation? As a family court counselor, the helper would be responsible for helping the family understand and then change its behaviors.

Perhaps it is clear now why the helper's understanding must remain tentative. There are many ways of understanding behavior, from the moral to the biological. There is a true continuum of influences on behavior as well, ranging from broad political and social events to the occurrences in a specific household. But lest the helper feel as though there is little chance to *truly* understand another person, it must be remembered that the helper does have a further goal in understanding. That goal is to eventually enable the helpee to change the situation in some way. In other words, the helper's way of understanding has a certain requirement: *that it enable change.*[1] So, while understanding current political and economic conditions is important, it is irrelevant as far as change for some helpees is concerned. The helper must try to understand at a level from which he or she can be helpful. Being helpful, to our minds, means creating a situation that fosters the development of adaptive behaviors relevant to the issues at hand. This is not always so easy, and many helpers become discouraged if they feel as though factors beyond their (and their helpees') control are creating or perpetuating problems. Unemployment, reflecting an economic slump, may have severe effects on individuals and their families. Helpers can still help, but they cannot create jobs.

To help, the helper must work to understand the helpee's "proximal" environment, those forces which are *directly* influencing the helpee's behavior. To do this, the helper must first understand the helpee's communication during the helping process.

THE PROCESS OF UNDERSTANDING

In order to understand, the helper must remain attentive both to details and to general impressions while working with the helpee. In a way, a helper must maintain a quiet but active *attitude of disbelief:* the helper must be alert, wondering, and doubtful. In this way, the helper will be able to discern important areas of concern. The helper charts each signal, thinks about it, and tries to identify its meaning and implications. This may take weeks or it may take seconds. Helpers must become skilled at identifying messages and judging their importance and relevance to the helpee's situation.

Understanding requires two complementary sets of skills. The first set is termed *global understanding.* At this level, helpers seek behavioral

---

[1] It is, of course, possible that no change is called for. The process of understanding, then, should have revealed this, and helping would involve developing helpee understanding and acceptance of the no-change situation.

and verbal impressions that can be classified into tentative descriptions by which to broadly understand the helpee's messages. These descriptions are of the feelings the helpee is conveying through both words and actions. The second set is more complex and is termed *deep understanding*. At this level, helpers seek to identify and explore specific helpee messages. There are five component skills involved in deep understanding: (1) identification of messages, (2) bringing the message to awareness, (3) exploration of meaning, (4) grasping the significance of the message, and (5) constructive collaboration.

Here is an example. A caseworker employed by a residential school for legally identified delinquent youngsters was in charge of a 16-year-old's court hearing. The caseworker discussed the upcoming hearing with Lida, stressing the importance of presenting a respectful demeanor with the particular judge who was to preside, since all the caseworkers and many of the teenagers had experience with the gruff and blustery man in charge of the court. Indeed, Lida had heard reports from her peers and had herself initiated the discussion about clothes and manner. Yet on the morning of her hearing, Lida showed up dressed most inappropriately. To use her terms, she "dolled herself up" in a low-cut, tunic style, red satin dress over a black satin skirt and tights and had put on the highest platform-heeled shoes she could find—red with black polka dots. Her hair was arranged in evening style, with ringlets hanging provocatively over her ears. Lastly, she selected bright flashy jewelry to complete her outfit. Lida also adopted a different way of walking from her usual, more direct style, bumping and grinding along, and she had decided to chew five sticks of gum at once. The caseworker was taken aback by Lida's appearance and manner. She didn't know quite how to understand this radical departure from Lida's own plans; she was perplexed by Lida's costume and manner of walking and talking. She quickly drew together her observations of Lida's behavior in order to be able to discuss her reactions constructively with her. The caseworker made a mental list of her impressions: cocky, arrogant, flashy, provocative. She then asked herself, "What is Lida trying to say? How do her verbalizations fit with her nonverbals?" She realized that, while her first impressions had validity, she could understand Lida's behavior in somewhat different terms as well. She described Lida's feelings as defensive, manipulative, and anxious. As they talked on the way to the hearing, the caseworker used these organizers to help her identify significant messages from Lida regarding the court appearance and her surprising costume. Several messages came through; of particular importance were a group of statements about Lida's mother. The caseworker sensed that Lida was fuming. As the caseworker tentatively conveyed the message, Lida disclosed that she was very angry at her mother and wanted to shock and hurt her. Knowing that her mother was going to be at the hearing, Lida decided to go all out in exactly the way her mother had warned her *not* to do just the day before. Lida recognized belatedly that she was also hurting herself and agreed that there might be other ways of handling her anger toward her mother. The caseworker's complementary use of global and deeper understanding, then, provided a foundation for an effective discussion with Lida and aided the helper in responding sensitively to the girl. To do so, the caseworker had to call on the component skills of both global and deeper levels of understanding.

GLOBAL UNDERSTANDING

For effective understanding, Danish, D'Augelli, and Hauer (1980) have identified four necessary behaviors. These are:

1. to observe what the helpee does;
2. to hear what the helpee says and how it's said;
3. to feel how the helpee feels;
4. to sense what the helpee has not said but may wish to say.

Both global and deep understanding ask the helper to engage in these four processes. The differences between the two levels of understanding lie in their goals. For global understanding, the helper is concerned with forming broad impressions in order to identify general messages. These general messages provide tentative keys to more specific helpee concerns, while offering useful information themselves regarding broad areas of concern and patterns of response. For deep understanding, the helper's concern is to delve into specific meanings of stated and unstated helpee messages. Doing so enables wider self-exploration of great depth and provides the foundation for formulating plans of action to enable change.

Global understanding depends on three component skills:

1. rapid observation,
2. impression forming, and
3. affective description.

The helper needs to be able to quickly but accurately scan the helpee's behavior. Then the helper must formulate the impressions he or she has received about the helpee on the basis of these observations. Lastly, the helper needs to organize these impressions into affective descriptions immediately useful to the helping process.

Rapid Observation

When we meet people, we naturally make note of several aspects of their appearance and demeanor. Some of us look first at style of dress. Others look at physical characteristics. Still others note manner of speaking. Helpers need to recognize their typical observation targets, polish these, and add new targets for a more complete set of clues.

The skill of rapid observation requires that the helper attend to all those elements of the helpee's nonverbal behavior. The helper must also take note of the helpee's use or lack of use of the various verbal responses described as helper responses. To proceed in global understanding, the helper must first be aware of these characteristics in the helpee's communication. So, the helper scans the helpee's behaviors, observes outstanding aspects of the helpee's self-presentation, and mentally takes note of these varied observations. The aware helper marks the helpee's general appearance, facial movements, limb movements, body posture, general verbal response style, and specific use of different verbal responses. These mental notes are then used to formulate impressions.

The skill of rapid observation is most consciously used when first meeting a helpee. Our initial observations of any other person are important cues for our understanding of the new relationship. We probably tend to be most observant of these structural details when we know least about the other person in terms of spoken feelings and disclosures. Rapid observation is also called upon in subsequent meetings with the same helpee, as the initial source of data for understanding the current relationship and new developments.

Impression Forming

First impressions are based on various aspects of our observations of others. After first meeting someone, we all catch ourselves saying such things as "She's a go-getter" or "He's nice, but a bit flaky." In a sense, we are making judgments about the other. Often, we feel uncomfortable doing so. In our society, we are generally admonished not to base our opinions of people on our first, quickly produced impressions of them. Somehow it doesn't seem fair to judge people on the basis of minimal information. Indeed, it isn't fair and impressions frequently change as we get to know the person better. We need to be flexible and mature enough to allow ourselves to be open to new ways of seeing the person. But first impressions *do* affect our ways of understanding others and how one initially comes across has an undeniable impact on subsequent interaction.

In helping, the same general principles hold true. First impressions are important. How the helper perceives the helpee has some impact on the helping interaction. At the same time, these impressions are recognized as *tentative* ways of understanding the helpee. One important difference exists, however; in helping, articulating one's impressions of the helpee is done for a very specific purpose. This is to enable the helper to organize his or her global understanding of the helpee so as to have initial hypotheses to work with in progressing in the helping process. These impressions are used, then, to specify descriptions and provide leads for the helper to work with in identifying important helpee messages.

The formulation of impressions draws from the details of manner and style observed, tying together the behaviors in meaningful ways. The helper works to pull together the observations in terms of a tentative meaning. For instance, a helper may observe that a helpee maintains eye contact, discloses past inadequacies, and leans forward. The helper's impressions are: sensitive, perhaps seductive. The helper will next want to check further on the fit of these impressions, in terms of the congruence of the helpee's affective communications, both verbal and nonverbal.

Affective Description

This last component of global understanding, affective description, is perhaps best reviewed as a more elaborated process of impression forming. In other words, affective description of a helpee's communications to the helper is largely a process of reformulating initial impressions on the basis of further information. The helpee's behaviors during an entire interaction are the data for affective description. What the helper attempts to do to broaden global understanding at this stage is to organize the observed details and impressions into *patterns*. The task of affective description is to summarize the helpee's overall affective demeanor.

Perhaps the main differences between impression forming and affective description are these:

1. Impressions can be and usually are based on less information than are affective descriptions.
2. Impressions need not be affectively stated, but affective descriptions must be.
3. Impressions tend to carry helper biases, while affective descriptions remain free of it.

Impressions tend to be made on the basis of the helper's own reactions to the helpee's behavior and may sometimes even be judgmental. The helper responds to the helpee in terms of his or her own needs or prior experiences with similar situations. Affective description, on the other hand, is meant to be free from such possible distortion. The helper avoids imposing his or her own feelings or situation on the helpee's behavior.

Affective description, then, is the helper's interpretation of the helpee's general emotional messages. By connecting the observations in patterns and discarding erroneous interpretations, the helper is able to summarize tentatively the significant broad themes emerging from the current interaction. To use our previous examples of the possibly sensitive/possibly seductive helpee, we might find that both are valid impressions when the helpee's behavior is further analyzed. Additional information suggested that useful affective descriptions are: caring, manipulative, and sensitive. The seductiveness is understood in broader terms, in particular that the helpee is generally manipulative of the situation. The helpee's sensitivity is reconfirmed and broadened to include warm and caring. The helper will want to use this information in the process of deep understanding, possibly to explore the contradictions that a manipulative but sensitive person may present. Affective description thus offers leads to work with in further understanding.

AN EXAMPLE

Think about this illustration of global understanding. A nutritionist working with an overweight adolescent boy found himself in a quandary. He had met twice with Roger, who had been referred by his school nurse and his own physician, both of whom viewed his increased blood pressure as a danger signal requiring intervention. The nutritionist's first thoughts were that this would be a straightforward consultation. After all, since Roger was medically cleared to lose a certain amount of weight and his parents were supportive, the task of the helper was simply to plan a weight control program fitted to the boy's taste in food, nutritional needs, and activity level. To plan the change program, the nutritionist would have to inquire about Roger's preferences and prepare meals and activity plans he could live with. Yet something was wrong. The nutritionist asked the usual questions, but received short replies, insufficient to build a weight control program. It wasn't that Roger was monosyllabic or hostile, but his answers were not adequate. The nutritionist decided to think through this dilemma; he wanted to help the child as best he could, and he also felt some challenge.

As he thought about the two meetings he had held with the boy, the nutritionist recalled his first impressions. Roger had struck him as a nice kid, but aloof and maybe a bit angry at the world. At their first meeting, he remembered, he had offered his hand in greeting and Roger shook it but didn't look at him. The nutritionist decided to list other actions which made him think that Roger was aloof. The boy sat rigidly, with his body turned at an angle away from the nutritionist. He generally looked down when the nutritionist spoke. He kept his hands stiffly on the arms of the chair and didn't gesture at all. Occasionally, though, his face would screw up at something the nutritionist said, and a couple of times he had stuck out his lower lip in a pouting way. But he did seem to be a nice boy. He smiled at times and laughed at the nutritionist's jokes, even though he quickly checked himself. And he spoke in an even voice, without harshness or sarcasm—that is, until the second session. At that meeting, some of Roger's responses *had* been sarcastic, the nutritionist recalled. He also remembered that Roger kept shaking his foot, even though he held the rest of his body rather stiffly. He may have blushed when the nutritionist suggested that girls would find him very attractive once he lost weight. All in all, the nutritionist decided, Roger acted similarly both times but did seem to have a bigger chip on his shoulder the second time. Perhaps, he thought, there was a way of putting together these broad clues, organizing his thinking about Roger and Roger's needs in a more directed way.

As he checked out his first impressions, the nutritionist realized that what he took to be aloofness could well be nervousness. Roger was probably nervous about coming for help and apparently was anxious about meeting with a helper to discuss his eating problems. The nutritionist remembered that Roger had indeed said that he didn't know what to expect; often when helpees say that, they actually have an image in their minds about what the helping relationship will be about. All Roger's behavioral cues were signals of anxiety. Yes, *nervous* and *anxious* were useful affective descriptions of Roger's behavior at these sessions. Roger was not necessarily a withdrawn person, but rather had some general anxieties about what he was going to become involved in at the center. His reluctance to disclose was probably *guardedness,* keeping himself reserved until he felt more comfortable and trusting in the relationship.

But there was some other general feeling which the nutritionist had first viewed as anger; perhaps that first impression could be better understood as embarrassment. Looking down, blushing, talking sarcastically at times could more accurately be expressions of embarrassment at being overweight and at being sent to an agency to deal with the problem. He might have even gotten teased by friends and felt ashamed as well as embarrassed. The nutritionist thought to himself that this affective description was a useful hypothesis to go on; to check it out would require deeper understanding to complement his more informed global understanding. He wished he had been more attuned to Roger's feelings during their meetings, but recognized that his eagerness to help plan the new program with Roger had overshadowed his awareness of issues other than nutritional ones. After thinking it through, however, the nutritionist felt comfortable knowing that he would use his global understanding to really listen to Roger at the upcoming meeting and would be able to help Roger work through some of his emotional responses to the situation as well as his nutritional responses.

DEEP UNDERSTANDING

Identifying Messages

Message identification is the first task in the process of deep understanding. This involves listening for messages, a continued process in all helping relationships. As in rapid observation, you "listen" with your ears, with your eyes, with your body, and with your mind. All parts of you are involved in the listening process. As we pointed out earlier, your "self" is an important tool in the developing of understanding in helping relationships. Your self *must* be brought to bear on the task of listening for messages.

An example will clarify this point. The example we shall use involves a helper in a one-to-one helping situation, although the deep understanding process is not limited to such circumstances; nor is the use of deep understanding limited to counseling settings. Rather, it is also applicable to helping interactions involving police officers engaged in crisis intervention, nurses attending to patients in medical hospitals, teachers working with students from preschool through college, doctors treating clients for cuts and bruises, lawyers discussing issues with their clients, and so on.

Consider working with a woman who is saying to you: "Somehow people don't seem to like me. It upsets me, but I don't think many people can stand being with me for any length of time." Listening to the remark, you ponder your own feelings at that moment. Your mind notes that your body feels tense and tight. Once you recognize your own response to this individual, you ask yourself why you feel the way you do. You might find yourself thinking, "Well, I feel tense when I'm around people who constantly question their worth to others, who seem obsessive about it." Meanwhile, your eyes have noted that the woman herself looks tense. She is sitting stiffly upright in her chair, her mouth is set and hard, and she is clutching the arms of the chair. Your ears have heard a few messages, as you think about what she has said and how she has said it. And emotionally you feel some dislike; you are not feeling comfortable enough to want to be helpful.

As you can see, you listen for messages in the person's physical behavior, in vocal tone and quality, in silence as well as in words. You also attend to your own physical responses, your gut-level indications of feelings, and your own thoughts. And, later on, you plan your use of these observations.

How does the helper *identify messages*? Doing so involves a decoding process. In listening for messages, you have begun to identify them. In *questioning* a message—asking whether the message you think you picked up is actually a message—you are beginning to decode it.

Identifying a message as such requires further decoding. This aspect of the process is called *restatement*. That is, you think back to the words you heard, the gesture you observed—the source or sources of the message—and you restate the message to yourself.

Take the example of the woman discussed above. We remember that she said "Somehow people don't seem to like me. It upsets me, but I don't think many people can stand being with me for any length of time." A simple restatement would be: "People dislike me and don't spend much time with me." This essentially paraphrases her thought. We can go one step beyond this simple restatement. What are some *other ideas* that this woman may be expressing? Restating her words again, we might say that she communicated the following concerns: "People do not seem interested in me as a person and are uncomfortable with me."

Now ask yourself: *why* did she say this at *this particular moment? Survey the context* for the communication. Attend to the proximal environment for the client's behavior. The immediate context is the ongoing session involving you as helper and your client. This is the "here-and-now" of your helping relationship. Surveying the context means examining the here-and-now process of that relationship: what has been happening between you and the helpee? Being alert to the process of your helping relationships is fundamental to effective helping.

What was the context for this helpee's message? In fact, you now recognize that you had shifted your body away from her and indeed had moved your chair as well. She initially had seated herself at some distance from you, but had moved closer as the session progressed. Further, she had talked a great deal, but about mostly mundane things and you found yourself bored and restless. Your interjections became less frequent. This, then, was the current context for her communication—the physical, interpersonal, and emotional environment. You suspect, then, that the helpee was responding very directly to what was occurring between you and her. She was responding to your impatience, as she perceived your behavior, and to her own interpersonal anxieties.

Surveying the context may also profitably include some attention to relevant client interactions outside the helping relationship. The most important are those immediately preceding the meeting, the real world of families, friends, work, schools, and neighborhoods. Also worth noting are the histories of the helpee's significant relationships. Are there repetitive patterns? Are your responses to the helpee similar to others' responses? Is your relationship echoing others the helpee has experienced? The congruence and the discrepancies are worth exploring in resolving the client's concerns. The outside context in this case reflects disharmony in the woman's relationship with fellow workers but a close marital relationship.

By surveying the here-and-now and the relevant outside context for the communication, you take decoding a bit further. Doing so gives the helper a broader perspective in which to comprehend and begin to interpret the message.

At this point, the helper may make an initial interpretation. You think to yourself: "Okay, she was feeling my boredom and restlessness. What might she be asking for in making her statements?" That is, you seek the underlying emotional message and translate it into words. One tentative interpretation, spoken to yourself at this point, is that this woman wants reassurance from you, the helper. She may have been really saying: "Please tell me that it's okay for me to be here. Tell me that you accept me."

Other interpretations are possible and the helper should consider several. This helpee may be asking if the helper likes her. Or, alternatively, the helpee may be saying that she herself is uncomfortable with the helper at that moment. Considering the words, the nonverbal behaviors, and the current context permits formulation of several tentative hypotheses, initial ways of understanding the helpee's message.

So far, the process of understanding has been as follows: you have identified the message, decoded it as a message by restating it, surveyed the context, and reflected on several tentative interpretations. Phase I, identifying the message, has involved clarification of the communication and emotional understanding of the meaning. Phase II in the understanding process is that of bringing the message to awareness.

Bringing the Message to Awareness

As we stressed earlier, the understanding process is a constant process of discovery. *Bringing the message to the client's awareness* is one aspect of the process of discovery. For one thing, the helper is making explicit some of the person's own feelings and needs. For another, the helper and client can discover useful and important information about the helpee's reactions to the helper's awareness-building. Those reactions contain important messages to be identified. It is truly a constant process.

When we discuss bringing the message to awareness, we mean bringing it to the helpee's attention. In the process of identifying the message, it has been brought to the *helper's* awareness. Note, however, that the helper may not always identify and hence become aware of a message at the immediate moment it is delivered. Often the helper becomes aware of messages only later on, when thinking back over the meeting—the words, gestures, remembered feelings, and so on. However, many messages are heard and decoded during a meeting. How does the helper bring a message to the helpee's awareness?

There are a variety of approaches. All require sensitivity to the helpee's feelings and integrity as a person. The helper should play an active role, not to show that he or she is smart or skeptical, but literally to make sure that he or she understands what is being told—and to explore the message.

One of the key rules is *to be tentative*. As a helper, it is true that you are "expert" in some ways. But this does not insure that your interpretations are necessarily correct. Remember they are hypotheses, or tentative statements that need to be tested. One of the first tests is that of checking out your hypotheses with the helpee.

Given our example of the woman helpee, the helper might decide to check out the second interpretation first, that interpretation being that the helpee is asking if the helper likes her. You as helper might say something like this: "I find myself wondering, when you tell me people dislike you, whether you're saying something along these lines: 'I don't seem to belong here. I'm uncomfortable. I wonder what you think of me.' Does this make any sense to you?" In making this observation, the helper has brought the message of the helpee's behavior to her awareness. It is now ready to be explored for its possible meanings, the next issue in the understanding process.

One issue in awareness-building needs to be addressed before going on—*timing*. That is, when does the helper bring an unstated message to a helpee's awareness? Timing is a difficult and complex aspect of helping; since no guidelines exist, it has long been a problem. A police officer at the scene of a family quarrel may find it appropriate to restate the emotional messages openly communicated as, for example, "Both of you are furious right now—you're feeling explosive." However, the officer may choose *not* to further interpret the message being communicated, such as "You seem to be questioning your relationship, but don't know how to explore it." If the couple was engaged in counseling at a family consultation clinic when they broke out into quarreling, bringing the latter to attention might well be apt.

Unfortunately, it is extraordinarily difficult to tell new helpers when to raise issues, especially sensitive ones. Much depends on the nature of the helping relationship. That is why surveying the context is so important and must at least begin while the message is happening. Another aspect of timing involves the sensitivity of the message or the issue involved. Sensitivity refers to the degree of *psychological threat* it holds for the helpee. The emotional charge of an issue must therefore be considered. As a helper, you must learn to take the temperature of an issue.

A third aspect of timing involves relevance. How important is the message to the helping process at that moment? If it is relevant to the discussion at hand, as in our example, then it is useful to raise it then and there. If it is relevant to the continuation of the helping relationship, it is probably important to bring it to awareness at that time. However, if it is relevant to a goal not yet being worked on, the helper must keep it in mind and raise it at that point in the relationship when it is meaningful. Likewise, hold the message in check if it brings up new issues distracting to the concerns being explored. For example, an employment counselor may be discussing a helpee's career goals when the helpee gives the counselor a message implying marital conflicts. It is unlikely that bringing the message to awareness at that particular time will be constructive.

You can see that our message here is one of sensitivity and perceptiveness. You as helper must develop a sense of timing. This skill comes largely from experience. It grows out of observations about helpees' responses and out of the helper's increasing understanding of the understanding process itself. Remember the general guidelines and test out your hypotheses. Above all, consider the helpee as a person and keep in mind the helping goals toward which you both are working. If you decide to test your hypotheses immediately and bring the message to awareness, you will enter Phase III of the understanding process, exploring the message with the helpee. If not, you can explore it by going through several phases of the understanding process on your own, later retracing steps when and if you do bring the message to helpee awareness.

Exploration of Meaning

In this aspect of the understanding process, the helper is engaged in the *redefinition* and *extension* of the helpee's message. This helping activity really begins in the initial interpretation step. As you review the examples below, it will be clear that the words of the helpee are redefined beyond their face value. The helpee's words are explored for many levels of meaning. It's not that the communication as presented is not meaningful at face value; rather, we suggest that many communications contain much meaning, and part of the work in helping is to ferret out the relevant meaning to further illuminate and promote the goals of the helping relationship. At the least, clarification and affirmation of meaning will occur. The most constructive exploration of meaning is carried out collaboratively, with helper and helpee picking their way carefully over an unpaved road and paving the way for further understanding.

In order to open the door for exploration of meaning, the helper must first state an initial interpretation of the message. This statement of meaning most frequently, though not always, involves an affective analysis of the message and hence will most often be an affective response. Immediately following the redefinition of the helper's original communication, whether it stems from verbal, vocal, gestural, or other sources, the helper employs a *"door opening" response*. A door opener is a response that gives the other person an opportunity to react to the helper *without* the imposition of the helper's judgment or feelings. They are invitations to talk. Examples of common door openers are:

"How does that strike you?"
"What are your thoughts on this?"
"Does that make some sense to you?"
"Want to tell me about it?"
"Let's talk about these feelings."
"Can you clarify this for me?"

At this point, the helpee will respond. The helper's role, therefore, becomes that of alert observer and (again) message identifier.

If the helpee is unwilling or unable to start the exploration, several possibilities exist. First, the helper's way of stating the redefinition may not have been comprehensible to the individual because of word choice. If so, a restatement is in order. Second, it is possible that the helper's manner of opening the door caused problems. Insincere or evaluatively-toned door-opening delivery is likely to put the helpee on guard. The helpee will probably react by denying the helper's suggestion without reflection on it. Third, the interpretation the helper selects to explore first may simply be wrong. It may be inappropriate, inaccurate, or perhaps poorly timed.

A simple restatement of the message may sometimes be more helpful than an initial interpretation. Restatement provides a slightly modified frame of reference for exploration; interpretation provides an alternate way of understanding the message. A nurse speaking with a patient soon to undergo open-heart surgery might respond to the patient's tension and irritability by restatement of the message: "You're feeling touchy right now. Want to talk?" If the patient opens the exploration of her fright, the nurse later might offer an initial interpretation, "You're scared about the operation." Constructive exploration depends upon timing, particularly the helpee's ability to hear and to use the restatement and interpretations.

When the helpee does respond to the door-opener, the most facilitative helper action is the use of skillful continuing responses. Help the individual continue to explore. This is the key to Phase III of the understanding process. At times, the helper may give a relevant affective response; at other times, an appropriate open question may be in order. The goal is meaningful, in-depth exploration of the message to foster deep understanding. Remember that interpretations are hypotheses. They may be accepted, revised, discarded, or replaced, depending upon the fruitful exploration of meaning.

Let's return to the helper's statement made in bringing the message to awareness of the woman helpee: "I find myself wondering, when you tell me people dislike you, whether you're saying something along these lines: 'I don't seem to belong here. I'm uncomfortable. I wonder what you think of me.' Does this make any sense to you?"

In asking the client whether the interpreted restatement has any meaning for her, the helper opens the door for exploration of the message in its alternative *or* multi-level meanings. Why don't we carry on this hypothesized helping interaction and see where it leads?

The helpee becomes engaged in the exploration with the helper when the helper opens the door.[2] This woman client might respond to the tentative interpretation in any number of ways, for instance:

Response 1: "Well, it does make sense to me, now that you put it *that* way."

Response 2: "You've gotta be kidding. No, I don't care what you—or others—think of me."

Response 3: "Yeah, I suppose it does make sense. I wouldn't have said that I care about what you think. But I guess I do want to be liked by you."

All are possible responses and mark the beginning of the exploration of meaning. Possible helper responses that might follow these helpee statements and carry the exploration along are as follows.

Helper 1: "My rephrasing your thoughts made sense of your feelings."

Helper 2: "What I think isn't important to you."

Helper 3: "You are concerned about how others feel about you and right now you're wondering about my reaction."

Let's hypothesize the woman's responses to these helper statements. Then we will examine the interactions for their relevance to the skill of exploring alternative meanings to helpee messages.

Response 1: "Mmhmm, it does make sense. I can see I was feeling really up-tight. Even my body was stiff, tight. I think I wished that you'd give me an out. But I was also wishing that you'd like me."

Response 2: "I wouldn't say that. I just don't put a lot of stock into other people's feelings."

Response 3: "Yes, that's it. I know you don't really know me yet; still I hope you like me and that you want to help me."

In each response, there is evidence of several layers of meaning which the helper has elicited.

---

[2] Helpees sometimes open the door to exploration of meaning themselves. Some helpees are alert to possible alternative messages in their behavior and spend time puzzling them out. The helper's task here becomes one of guiding the exploration constructively.

Examine the alternative definitions of the original message which were raised in the three respective responses. They raise the following possible meanings, respectively.

Response 1	Response 2	Response 3
1. Feeling anxious in the relationship	1. Disinterest in the helper's personal response to her	1. Eagerness to be known (and get to know)
2. Wishing the helper to provide an out	2. Defensiveness regarding others' feelings	2. Wanting to be liked
3. Wishing the helper to like her	3. Anxiety in relationships	3. Concern that she can be helped

As you can see, there are both similarities and differences in the alternative meanings of each response's message. The exploratory redefinitions of the messages recognized discomfort and anxiety in relationships in the messages of two responses (1 and 2); the wish to be liked and accepted is common to another pair of responses (1 and 3). Yet all three *sets* of possible meanings are distinct. Helpers who are skillful in deep understanding will continue to explore with the helpee the distinctive meanings of messages.

Grasping the Significance of a Message

Narrowing down the major significance of a message is the next step. It is a difficult process, but the responsibility is shared with the helpee, as both helper and helpee work toward sensing and identifying the most important aspects of the message. *Grasping the significance of a message,* Phase IV, is the aspect of deep understanding that people most often identify with definitions of "understanding." Stop and think for a moment about how you would define understanding. You may have thought to yourself, "Well, understanding involves comprehending the meaning of a message or communication." When one arrives at an understanding, one has achieved a grasp of the nature, the significance, or the explanation of something. This aspect of the process then involves narrowing down the initial interpretations and possible alternative meanings that have been explored earlier. Narrowing down refers to crystallizing those aspects of meaning that seem to have the greatest present relevance to the attainment of helping goals.

How does a helper go about working with a helpee to ascertain the primary relevance of the message? Narrowing and grasping the significance entails *summarizing feelings, confronting* the helpee, and reaching a *working hypothesis.* To illustrate, we shall review the interaction with Response 1. In this hypothesized situation, the interchange raised the following alternative meanings: (1) feeling anxious in the relationship,

(2) wishing the helper to provide an out, and (3) wishing the helper to like her.

The helper, in ending Phase III and beginning Phase IV of the understanding process, proceeds to *summarize the possible meanings in the helpee's message.* The helper might say "You seem to be feeling several things all at once: tension, a desire to leave, and a desire to be liked."

In introducing the search for major current significance, the helper would go one step further to *begin to confront* the helpee. For example: "You are feeling uncertain about being here. I wonder, though, what your most intense feeling is." In gently confronting, the helper begins to focus attention on *predominating* feelings and other aspects of the message, including the helpee's life outside the helping relationship. In such confrontation, the helper utilizes skills for affective and informational clarification. The purpose of this is to narrow down the alternatives until both helper and helpee agree upon a *working hypothesis* of the major significance of the message. It is called a "working" hypothesis because it is used to pursue the helping goals at that moment.

We will use our example to further illustrate this process. Following the confrontive statement quoted above, the client replies:

Helpee: "That's really hard to say. I'm not sure which of my feelings is my primary one."

Helper: "You're finding it difficult to pinpoint which feeling is the most intense at this time."

Helpee: "Yes."

Helper: "It is hard to separate our feelings. But it's important to try so that we can work effectively. Maybe it'd be helpful to think about it this way: what is your major concern right now?"

Helpee: "When you put it that way, I guess I'm not much worried about feeling tense. I sort of expected to. I guess I'm really concerned about you and how you feel about me."

Helper: "You're worried that I may not like you."

Helpee: "Yes. I feel uncomfortable because I'm unsure what you think of me—no one seems to like me much and I sometimes feel I must be really an awful person."

Helper: "You'd like reassurance."

Helpee: "Mmhmm. I want you to like me."

Thus, the helpee has grasped the predominant message expressed much earlier in her statement "Somehow people don't seem to like me. It upsets me, but I don't think many people can stand being with me for any length of time." She recognizes and now admits that she wants the helper to like her. Note that her original statement was not specific to the helping relationship. It by-passed the helper and stressed instead some general feelings about being disliked. In this sample of the understanding process, the helpee and helper have come a long way.

In the interchanges above, it is clear that the helper is using verbal helping behavior with purpose. The confrontation in narrowing down the significance can be very gentle, as in this example, or it can be more direct. The manner of confrontation will vary depending upon the helping relationship. Certain theories of helping suggest that offering gentle, affective probes or comments is the most facilitative helping stance. Others suggest that directive or even abrasive confrontations are most effective. Our position is that the former responses are more frequently accepted by helpees and therefore are preferable.

Of course, in our example, the path was fairly easy. And sometimes the process will unfold as easily. Other times, the process of deep understanding will be lengthier and more arduous. But the purposes and tasks are clear: to help the person in some way to sense, feel, and explicitly label the most important meaning and goals contained in his or her own message.

Constructive Collaboration

The understanding process is directed toward facilitating and working on *goal attainment*. Understanding for its own sake—to develop insight—often fails to be goal-directed. Yet insight can foster some discernible change, whether in thought or in overt verbal or physical behaviors. One example of insight effecting behavior change is common: people experience increasing difficulty in buttoning clothes and closing zippers and soon recognize that they have put on weight. They often decide to slim down. To do so requires some planning and habit change, and many people follow through and lose the extra weight. An example of insight leading to no change is unfortunately common. While it is clear that tobacco smoking is a primary factor in developing lung cancer, emphysema, and other lung diseases, many people ignore the evidence and continue to smoke. One often hears "I know it's bad for me. I know I'll probably get cancer. But I'm going to keep on smoking anyhow." Insight alone, therefore, is insufficient to promote behavior change.

Goal-directed understanding is aimed at ultimately effecting visible changes. *Using the insight for goal-directed work* is the aim of the understanding process. Recognize, however, that immediately visible changes are unlikely to occur. In using the understood meaning of a message, the helper works with the helpee to define the need or feeling in behavioral terms. Secondly, they work together to suggest ways of working on the need to reach the behavioral goal.

In our example, the helper might respond as follows to the woman's final working hypothesis, her statement of significance, which was:

Helpee: "Mmhmm. I want you to like me."
Helper: "So your wish at this moment is to hear from me about how I see you and how I feel about you."

Thus saying, the helper uses the helpee's insight to move toward some concrete, observable, and meaningful plan of action. In this case, the first step in that plan most logically involves feedback. This feedback will in itself raise messages for identification and exploration, while simultaneously providing definite and useful personal information to the client and the helper. The interaction might continue as follows.

Helpee: "Yes, I want to know how you feel about me as a person."
Helper: "Okay. That's fair. We've been meeting for three weeks now and I have had some difficulty in relating to you. I like you, yes, but I find it very difficult to accept your critical ways of seeing other people and events. That makes me uncomfortable. I also get uncomfortable with your reliance on tactics for getting your way. So I'm wondering if you behave critically with people you know."
Helpee: "I suppose I am critical. No, I know I am. Yeah, people think I'm snobbish and manipulative. I know I have high standards for others; yet I hold them for myself, too."
Helper: "You see yourself as very discerning, for yourself and others."
Helpee: "Yes. But I see that it does make people uncomfortable and annoyed."
Helper: "Even defensive."
Helpee: "I hadn't thought of that. I can see now that I must really turn off people although I don't intend to. I want them to see how intelligent I am, how worldly-wise. But I must come across as a snob."
Helper: "You're beginning to see aspects of your behavior you hadn't thought about before."
Helpee: "Yes."
Helper: "You can see some consequences of your behavior, even if unintentional. You dislike the results. What do you think you might do differently?"

At this point, the helper will be able to identify useful goals for the helpee to work toward. This phase involves collaborative work and resolution. It includes the definition of one or more goals to work toward in the helping relationship. It also entails developing a *plan of action* for attaining those goals. Thus, the helper leads the helpee through the understanding process, bringing the helper to awareness of her or his behavior and aiding the helpee to think through and work on different behavioral goals. The next chapter will discuss strategies for working on problems.

SUMMARY

The understanding process is a complex one. It is constantly being repeated during the course of a helping relationship. The process itself is a movement toward clarity of meaning. It first involves formulating a global understanding of the helpee's behavior. Next, deep understanding involves grasping the significance beyond the face value of a message. The meanings and unstated purposes of helpees' communications are explored and assessed for their relevance to the goals of the helping relationship. This holds for nurses working with patients, teachers working with students, police responding to crisis calls, caseworkers speaking with clients, and so on.

In understanding, you as helper are both an explorer and a researcher. You are alert for discoveries and are able to take them, comprehend them, and relate them to other already understood aspects of the relationship and the helpee's goals. The helper, thus, aids the helpee in searching out and discerning meaning.

In order to do so, the helper must be an alert observer as well as an active participant. Furthermore, helper behaviors are directed toward becoming thoroughly familiar with the feelings, ideas, character, and inclinations of your helpee. This is a critical point: the helper is able to *accurately* comprehend meaning and grasp significance only insofar as he or she is familiar with the helpee. While helper feelings and insights are intuitively helpful, the helper must base interpretations on *solid evidence*. That is, the helper develops working hypotheses on the basis of observations and helpee behavioral statements. Then the helper begins the process of checking it out or, in other words, hypothesis-testing. The goals of global and deep understanding involve using these hypotheses to move toward deeper helpee understanding and change.

THOUGHT QUESTIONS

1. Why is it helpful to be tentative in conclusions about helpees and their problems?
2. What are the advantages and disadvantages of first impressions in understanding others?

3. How does the helper encourage the helpee to gain an understanding of his or her situation?
4. Why are a helpee's feelings so important in the helper's attempt to understand?
5. How can a helper's biases and needs interfere with understanding others?
6. Why is understanding a *broadening* process?
7. Can you understand helpees whose lives are extremely different from your own?
8. What helper verbal responses are involved in the process of understanding?
9. What types of problems or circumstances would it be hard for you to understand?
10. What is the role of interpretation in the process of understanding?

7
Helping Strategies

In Chapter 6, we discussed ways of understanding the messages helpees convey through their words and nonverbal behavior during a helping interaction. In this chapter, we will consider the *process of problem solving* in helping others. Many define helping as understanding and problem solving; we feel this is a simple but accurate definition. Before problem solving can occur, however, a complete analysis of the helpee's situation is called for, and this goes beyond the kind of understanding we described in the preceding chapter. The helper must appreciate the totality of the helpee's situation, not only his or her communication during a helping interaction. This kind of understanding is part of the problem-solving or change process and is itself a helping strategy. It includes an analysis of the problem, a plan to help resolve the problem, and a method to determine the success of the plan.

Common to all definitions of helping is the concept of *change*. Whether helping is resolving pressing problems, discussing life plans, or becoming more accepting of one's limitations, some change is implied. To accomplish this change, whatever it may be, helpers need tools. The helping skills we've described so far—nonverbal and verbal—lay the foundation for change and are tools for starting the helping process. They enable the helper to create a relationship in which change can be planned. In this chapter, helping *strategies* will be described. We will address this question: What does the helper do *after* having established a helping relationship and *after* understanding the messages communicated by a helpee? Take, for example, the case of an employment counselor working with an ex-convict. The counselor has heard the helpee's message to be: "I'm desperate for a job. I'm afraid I'll end up back in jail unless I get off the streets soon." The most skillful eye contact, the most empathic response, the most sincere disclosure will not resolve this problem. In addition to these skills, the helper needs a strategy, a set of plans to help this person achieve his or her stated goal—to find work.

Even before deciding upon plans, a helper needs a model of the problem-solving process in helping. There are many such models available—everything from Freud's complex psychoanalysis to a witch doctor's rationale for curative dances. We propose a rather simple model for helping, one that emphasizes the process of achieving helpee goals. The model is pictured in Figure 7-1.

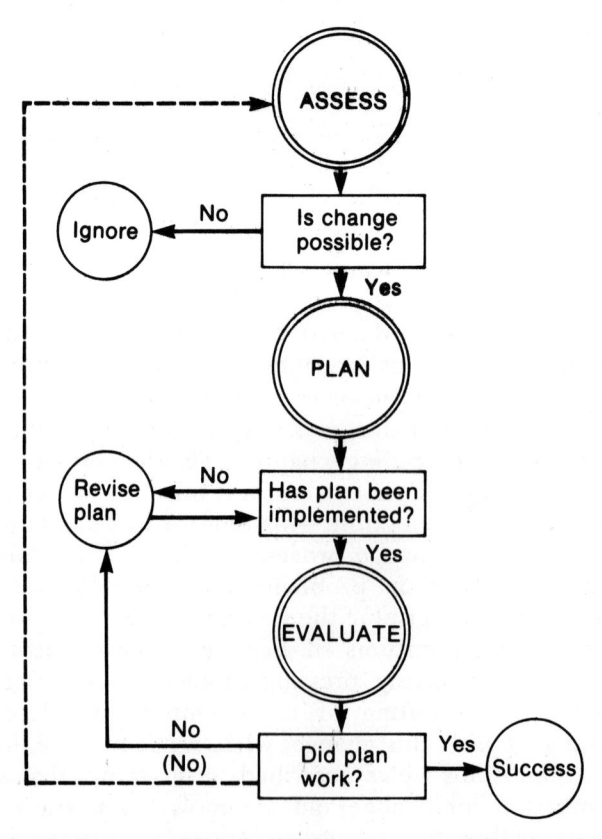

Figure 7-1. A model for helping that emphasizes the process of achieving helpee goals.

There are three major steps to the model:

1. *Assessment,* or understanding the problem;
2. *Planning,* or developing ways to resolve the problem; and
3. *Evaluation,* or determining the success of the plan.

These steps appear in the double circles. The rectangles contain questions the helper must ask himself or herself in proceeding through the model. Depending on the answer to a question, the helper can continue or must reconsider what's happened already.

Let us go through the model slowly. The helper and helpee first *assess* the helpee's situation, trying to gain an understanding of the causes of the problem and the factors maintaining the problem. This occurs most clearly in the Exploration (Stage 2) and Clarification (Stage 3) Stages of the helping process. Then the helper, along with the helpee, must come to a decision: Is change possible? This question is appropriate to the Integration Stage (Stage 4). The question, hardly as simple as it seems, can be restated as: With the resources available, is it likely that this helpee's situation can be modified to eliminate the problem? Is it a realistic expectation? If the answer is "no," the problem should be ignored. If "yes," the *planning* phase begins, starting the Program Planning Stage (Stage 5). After deciding on a plan, the helpee must try to put it into effect in the Action-Taking Stage (Stage 6). Another important question then occurs: Has the plan been implemented? Was the agreed-upon plan actually tried? If not, the plan needs revision to allow the helpee to try it. If it has been tried, then it is *evaluated*: Did it work? This occurs in the Reviewing Stage (Stage 7). If the evaluation is positive, success! If not, several choices remain. Perhaps the first is to revise the plan; after doing this, another evaluation occurs. A second choice is to *reassess* the situation. In this case, the helper is essentially saying "We have tried to resolve the wrong problem. I need to clarify my understanding of the helpee's problem and work toward a more accurate assessment." Because this decision is a major one, it is represented in the model by dotted lines.

Let us look at a brief example. A college student comes to a counseling service complaining of poor school work. After spending considerable time with this helpee, the helper determines that the student's problem in studying is a result of frustration in making friends, particularly opposite-sex friends. Thus, the helper has *assessed* the problem after gathering information and putting together impressions of the helpee. In discussing this analysis with the helpee, the helper agrees that change is possible and works with the helpee on a *plan*. The helper assigns the student the task of making two new opposite-sex friends a week. At their next meeting, the helper learns that the helpee was unable to implement the plan, since the helpee was too anxious to approach another person. A revised plan is designed that is easier to accomplish—talking to someone in a class during the next week. This plan is successful, and the helpee reports a sense of accomplishment in making one new friend. The helping relationship would not stop here, however, since the helpee has only begun to increase the number of friendships desired. But each time the helper and helpee set a goal and make a plan for the helpee, this general helping strategy should be followed.

This general model represents the set of decisions a helper makes during the process of helping. All of the specific decisions need not formally be discussed with the helpee, but the helper does need to have the answers. That is, many of the strategic means to the goals will be helper decisions, based upon learned skills, but the helper must be able to discuss the rationale of each one. Perhaps the most unusual aspect of this model is the evaluation. Many helpers do not look carefully at the outcome of their work and see their responsibility as ending with planning change. Our model strongly opposes this perspective and considers evaluation as *part* of helping. The remainder of this chapter will describe the details of this model. The three main components—Assessment, Planning, and Evaluation—will be presented in turn.

ASSESSMENT

The Assessment phase of the helping process concerns two questions: (1) What is the helpee's problem? and (2) Why did the problem occur, and what causes the problem to continue? To answer the first question, the helper must carefully *describe* the helpee's problem; to answer the second, the helper must *explain* the helpee's problem. Description of a helpee's problem includes specifying in detail *what* the problem is; explanation of the problem involves determining the reasons for the problem arising and what allows the problem to persist. In other words, the helper must create a picture of the helpee's current problem by providing all the details (observation) and by suggesting some causes for the problem (explanation). Answering both "what" and "why" questions demands considerable skill.

Describing a helpee's problem can be quite complex. For example, assume a harried father brings his adolescent son for help. The son has been found drunk in the family's basement. The father sees this as a problem; the son sees it as nothing unusually problematic. The helper's question is: what's the problem? A wife may complain to a marriage counselor that her husband is negligent, hardly ever praising her for her job accomplishments. The husband may feel like he's been a fine provider, that he's doing his job as he should. What does the helper do? Whose problem is it? An older businesswoman is distressed because her company is subtly encouraging her to retire. She has been unable to sleep, has been unable to eat, and contemplates suicide. What is her problem?

In an objective sense, there is no such thing as a problem. Rather, a person's behavior is given the *label* "problem" by someone who is troubled by that behavior. That person may be the individual himself or herself, someone close to the individual (a "significant other"), or a representative of society, like a teacher, police officer, or judge. Examples of labels provided by different people for the same situation appear below.

Label Provider   *Example*

Helpee
1. I'm really feeling depressed these days. Maybe I need help.
2. My wife and I are constantly fighting. I think we have a communication problem.
3. I'm really unhappy in this job. Maybe I should look into alternatives.

Significant Others
1. My husband has seemed really depressed the last few weeks. I'm quite concerned about him.
2. Joe has been very irritable with me. I never seem to say the right thing. Maybe he's been under too much stress at work.
3. I really wonder how Sally's adjusting to this new job. I don't think it's right for her.

Society[1]
1. People who feel sad for long periods of time can use help.
2. Spouses shouldn't argue vehemently and, if they do, should try to resolve their problems.
3. If you're not happy in your job, you should try to find another one.

These examples point out that the three perspectives may be similar—that there can be agreement between a person, the person's significant others, and society about applying the label "problem" to a behavior. There is general agreement that a very depressed person has a "problem" and needs help. However, disagreements are probably more likely in the real world of life problems. The most stressful differences are between a person and his or her significant others. When an individual's family considers some of his or her acts like the behaviors of a "disturbed" person, this will lead to considerable tension. Take, for example, a person who drinks to excess but does not admit it. His or her family may be living a life of extreme misery, since the person becomes abusive when intoxicated. However, the drinker may not wish to label his or her drinking as excessive, nor may he or she voluntarily seek help. What should a helper do if this person's spouse comes for assistance? What is the problem—the drinking or the drinker's in-

---

[1] Society "speaks" rather ambiguously; nonetheless, our culture provides messages about what is appropriate and inappropriate.

ability to recognize the severity of the situation or the family's current anguish?

The helper's role is no less complex when the person is in disagreement with society about certain behaviors. An historical example helps show this. A woman in the early 1900s might have been considered in need of help if she wanted to pursue a career. Her husband would find this peculiar, since his role was to be the career-oriented spouse. Her social circle might reject her because of her unusual aspirations. Her society, through its laws and customs, would provide little support. How should a helper operate if this woman came for assistance? The helper could legitimize the "problem" label given by the husband or the society; alternately, the helper could place the label on the social situation, thereby liberating this "victim" of social conservatism.

In describing the problem, helpers are involved in this labeling process. A helper may agree with a helpee that the problem is not really his or hers but rather society's. A helper might see the perspective of the helpee's significant others and disagree with the helpee's view. Or a helper may take the perspective of society in describing certain actions as problems. Without determining that there is a need for change, the helper has no right to interact further with the helpee. To decide that the helper has something to offer follows from the description of the problem. But how does the helper determine what the problem is?

The complexity of labeling is a result of the multiple factors that influence a person's behavior. We can view a person as the center of a set of concentric circles, each of which represents a set of influencing factors (see Figure 7-2). The closer circles have a more powerful influence than the more distant ones, and the effect of cultural factors may be quite indirect. All problems can be seen as residing somewhere within these circles. Below are several simple examples of how these factors are involved in problem behavior.

Influence	*Helpee Problem*
Nuclear Family	1. Family discourages helpee from studying by mocking homework. This leads to school failure.
	2. Parents have excessively rigid rules for adolescents, leading to rebelliousness and aggressiveness.
Extended Family	1. Grandparents reward young children for misbehavior, criticize parents' way of bringing up children.
	2. Relatives encourage family to place healthy older family member in nursing home since these relatives wish no "burden."
Social Institutions	1. Prisons perpetuate criminal behavior and make transition to routine life very difficult.

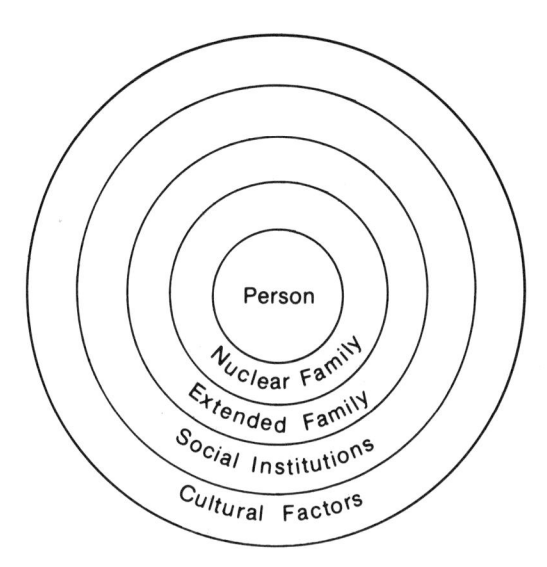

Figure 7-2. The individual is at the center of a set of influences.

	2. Unemployment benefit policies cause real hardships when benefits stop after a certain number of weeks.
Cultural Factors	1. By labeling homosexuality as a deviancy, society causes many people severe conflicts.
	2. By encouraging strong independence, society makes help-seeking difficult and makes people's problems worse.

Figure 7-2 helps illustrate another basic point: *that helpees' problems extend into their relationships to others and to society.* Upon exploring a "personal" concern of a helpee, many helpers discover that the concern results from problems in relationships with others—whether others are family members, employers, or society. Indeed, many problems are best seen as *relationship* problems, not *personal* problems. For example, it is probably a mistake to work individually with a husband complaining of marital dissatisfaction. It is also short-sighted to work with a disruptive school child without consulting with the child's teacher and parents. Helpers have become increasingly aware of the role of people's close relationships (especially families) in problem behavior. Since we agree that these are influences, we should also try to see the problem as residing in the relationship, not in the person.

Problem Description. With these ideas in mind, the helper must *describe* the problem. This should be done in behavioral terms. What does the person *actually say and do* that is a problem? Or what *doesn't* the person do that he or she should? Behavioral problem descriptions, then, involve *excesses* or *lacks*. A person who verbally abuses subordinates has a problem that can be called an excess; a person who does not date because of deficiencies in social skill has a lack. Remember, these terms are not evaluative and judgmental, but rather are *descriptive*. To complete the description, the helper needs to answer the following questions.

1. Under what circumstances does the problem occur?
2. How often does the problem occur?
3. Where does the problem occur?
4. Who is present when the problem occurs?
5. How long has the problem been occurring?
6. Who is concerned about the problem?

Taking as an example a child's temper tantrum, let's answer these descriptive questions.

1. The 4-year-old boy has a temper tantrum whenever he asks for a cookie and does not get one. He shrieks "Yes, yes, yes." He cries and sobs. He stamps the floor with his feet and then lies down on the floor and smacks it with his hands as well.
2. These tantrums occur four or five times a day.
3. The boy has these tantrums in the kitchen, for the most part. If mother takes child grocery shopping and he wants a cookie, he has tantrums in the store.
4. Mother is almost always present when he has tantrums. Father is frequently present, both at home and at the store. Sometimes the parents are together; most often, it is one or the other.
5. He has been having these tantrums for three or four months now. They seem to be increasing.
6. Both mother and father are concerned about this. It makes them angry and anxious. They worry that their son will hurt himself during one of these tantrums.

Problem Explanation. The helper next needs to turn to the issue of *explanation*. The explanation is not predominantly in terms of what past events may have "caused" the problem to happen but of what factors in the present seem to be associated with the occurrence of the problem behavior. A useful way of looking at explanation of problems is in terms of *antecedents* and *consequences*. In other words, the helper addresses two questions: (1) What occurred *before* the problem behavior that might have encouraged it? and (2) What occurs *following* the problem behavior that might cause it to continue? Typically, the first question concerns the *stimulus,* or *cue,* for the behavior; the second question concerns the *reward,* or *reinforcement,* of the behavior. Certain conditions or cues set the stage for the problem to occur. Equally important, problems continue for a reason. In other words, helpees are rewarded in some way after the problem behavior occurs.

Let's take an example using the same behavior, a child's temper tantrum. A helper working with a parent to decrease this problem behavior (assuming the helper has agreed with the parent that it *is* a problem) might observe the following.

1. Preceding each tantrum, the child makes a request for a cookie. The parent says no.
2. Following the tantrum, the parent gives the child the cookie and then picks up the child with great affection, acting as though he or she (the parent) felt guilty in bringing on the tantrum.

The helper could look at the sequence, or chain of events, as follows.

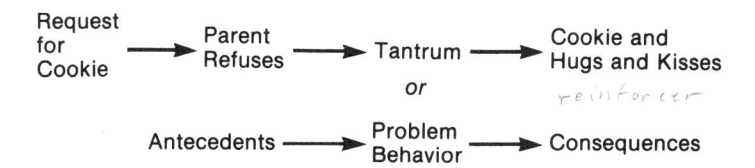

Request for Cookie → Parent Refuses → Tantrum → Cookie and Hugs and Kisses

Antecedents → Problem Behavior → Consequences

The request for the cookie started a chain of events that ended with the problem behavior. This request preceeded the problem and was associated with it. So the helper can begin to understand what *brings on* the problem. Furthermore, the mother and father help to perpetuate the problem by hugging and kissing the child, in addition to the direct reward of the cookie. So the helper also gains an understanding of why the tantrums *persist*—both parents inadvertently reward the child for the tantrums.

Thus, both the antecedents of problem behavior and the consequences must be understood. The helper needs to be especially sensitive to the consequences, since they serve to perpetuate the problem. Consequences can either be *positive reinforcers* that provide desirable rewards (such as affection, approval, money, or cookies) or *negative reinforcers* that stop ongoing unpleasant events. An example of a positive reinforcement of problem behavior is a drug-abusing teenager whose behavior is praised by his or her peer group. Negative reinforcement (*not* punishment) is more complicated. An example would be when a person develops headaches at social events in which he or she feels ill at ease; the headaches will reoccur if they serve to allow the person to leave such events early. In this way, the headaches serve a purpose and continue because of this.

PLANNING

After gaining an understanding of the helpee's situation, the helper begins to plan change with the helpee. This is not an easy process and, for most complex problems, takes time. In many ways, such planning is trial-and-error—trying to find a plan with which the helpee can live for some time. The plan must fit into the helpee's present life circumstances without undue burdens. Many helpers attempt to change their helpees' *lives* or their *personalities*. These goals, perhaps admirable, are very ambitious. Even if they were feasible, they would take immense time and effort. It is generally more reasonable to seek modest changes that will last, since such modest changes will make a real difference over time. A plan that calls for major change in a helpee's life simply may not work.

It is beyond the scope of an introduction to helping, as in this book, to present plans for solving the specific problems of helpees. Rather, we will discuss some general strategies for planning and then some helpful behavior change methods. Without more specific training, the general strategies are the problem-solving methods which the helper will use most in planning change with his or her helpees.

General Strategies

The following are some general principles of behavior change to keep in mind when planning. These may be considered general problem-solving strategies.

1. *Clarify the goal.* It is useful to consider what your helpee seeks to achieve. Often helpers dwell on problems and the current difficulties of a helpee and spend little time on careful consideration of exactly what the helpee *wants*. This approach is more future-oriented and gives both helper and helpee something to seek. Therefore, state the helpee's goal in positive, future terms instead of present problem terms. For example, a goal such as "to become more caring" is more helpful than "to avoid my usual hostility."

2. *Use behavioral terms.* How will your helpee know that he or she has achieved the goal? What are the behaviors associated with the goal? Be sure they are concrete behaviors ("be less critical of my friends; decrease put-down remarks I make"), not qualities or personality traits ("become a better friend").

3. *Keep in the present.* Avoid plans that dwell on past problems and "misdeeds." Focus on what has to be done now. Discuss the

present antecedents and consequences of the problem. ("I make many critical remarks when I am with my two closest friends, usually after they tell me something good is happening to them; then we end up talking about their weaknesses or disappointments.")

4. *Keep it positive.* Consider in a positive way what the helpee needs to do rather than emphasize what needs to be avoided. In other words, determine the helpee's present strengths and build on them. What could the helpee do better to resolve the problem? ("You seem to be able to recognize good qualities of these two friends, as we've explored the relationships. Perhaps a useful first step is for you to concentrate on their positive sides, on their strengths—things you like about them, actions you appreciate.")

5. *Be realistic.* Don't expect your helpee to do too much. Plan reasonable changes, not difficult ones. The helper's job should be to formulate a plan with the helpee that will most likely produce success, not failure. The goal can be such that effort is needed—it shouldn't be too easy—but it should be *attainable.* ("We can focus on identifying strengths and making positive remarks first. Then we might consider using 'personal messages' so you can make your feelings known in more constructive ways, rather than in hurtful ways as in put-downs.")

6. *Go in small steps.* Successful changes occur slowly, a little bit at a time. Be sure your plan doesn't call for extremely complicated behaviors at first. ("One way of beginning is to deliberately make two positive remarks each day with each of the two people, since you see each other daily.")

7. *Plan changes for the helpee's environment.* It's very important that the planning center on changes in the helpee's life situation, not changes only during the helping interaction. The helping role is to encourage change that will last, and it must occur in the helpee's natural environment. ("I'd like us to practice here first. You and I can role play to better recognize positive strengths and remark on them. Then I would like you to make such remarks in your friends' presence. We'll be able to talk about what happened, your feelings, and where to go from there.")

8. *Arrange support for changes.* The significant others of the helpee can be extremely helpful in supporting the changes the helpee is attempting. Of course, this is particularly true if the changes involve them directly. But even if they don't, these people (wives, husbands, parents, good friends, and so on) can encourage the helpee in very powerful ways. ("How would you feel about involving your roommate in helping you? For instance, telling her that you want to change certain behaviors and would like to enlist her assistance may be very valuable for you. She could monitor, via your report, the daily exercises and give you whatever reward you agree on for completing the particular goal.")

To illustrate how to use these planning principles, we will use an example. A young woman comes to a family planning clinic to be examined before beginning to use contraceptives. The helper she sees comes to realize that this is not a routine visit, but is really an attempt to solve some personal problems. The helpee expresses doubts about herself, her sexuality, and her stability. She feels that she should use contraception, but has no current relationship in which sexual involvement is likely. She feels very depressed about this and wonders why men do not seem to find her sexually attractive. In such a situation, many complex concerns are involved, of course, and we really can't know how to plan with this imaginary helpee. Still, here is how the helper might pursue some planning.

1. *Clarify the goal.* The helper should get this woman to consider what she *really* wants. Does she wish to attract men more? Does she want a lover? Does she want a long-term relationship? Does she want to be more assertive with men? To clarify the goal, the helper must move the helpee from continual discussion of her current woes to an honest statement of what she wants. Since many people are embarrassed to say what they want (perhaps this woman honestly wants a sexual relationship, no more and no less), it is not a simple matter of asking the helpee, "What do you want in this part of your life?" Rather, the helper needs to use continuing responses to help the person explore her goals. Most goals helpees have that give them conflict take time to clarify.

2. *Use behavioral terms.* It would be tempting to set the goal for this woman as "to come to terms with her own sexual needs." However, this is very vague and does not lead to action. So the goal must be in terms of what the helpee should really say or do. An example might be "to ask a man I work with whom I find attractive to go out to lunch" or "to tell my friend that I would like to make love with him." Once again, being this specific is not easy for helpees—it may be too threatening. On the other hand, to avoid honesty and clarity about what the helpee really wants to do is simply not helpful.

3. *Keep in the present.* This helpee may have had some very trying sexual encounters in the past which have left her scared of sexual involvement. It is useful to let the helpee discuss her understanding of her past in terms of how it influences her present circumstances. However, lengthy recollections of all of the events that led to her current situation are probably not helpful. This certainly does not lead to plans for change. So the helper might ask open questions like "Tell me about your current relationships with men" or "What is it about sex that scares you at this point?" or "What do you really want in a relationship right now?"

4. *Keep it positive.* It is extremely useful to talk about strengths, talents, and abilities. Let's say this woman has a negative view of her own value as a person and approaches others (men in particular) in a

very reserved, self-effacing manner, down-playing any of her achievements. The helper may usefully work to point out this person's obvious strengths by asking, "Tell me about your positive qualities—what do you do well?" These can be employed in the plan for change. A helpee who feels she is intimidated by large gatherings but who feels she is very at ease in a small group would best use the latter situation to get to know more men. A small dinner party would be preferable to going to a crowded social gathering. A helpee who is a potter or who studies modern literature would be wise to discuss these interests with people she knows. In other words, the helper must draw on who the person is in making plans.

5. *Be realistic.* Similar to point 4, this principle can make plans likely to succeed. For our helpee, the helper needs to ask what is a realistic goal. Should this helpee plan to meet a new man? ten new men? Should she expect to be involved in a "meaningful" (in her terms) relationship in a week? in three months? These questions can be answered only by a thorough understanding of the helpee—there are no standard answers to the question of what is "realistic." But it is best to set a goal that is modest and attainable vs. one that may be very attractive yet impossible to reach. This helpee should not, for example, plan to have dates every night, though that may be her fantasy.

6. *Go in small steps.* Any plan needs to be considered as a set of steps. A goal such as "to have two dates per week with interesting men" needs to be broken down into steps that will lead to the goal. For example, some steps might be: (1) make a list of men I'd like to meet, (2) consider how to make the initial contact, (3) call one man with a specific idea for a get-together.

7. *Plan changes for the helpee's environment.* This principle is a general one that pushes the helpee beyond the helping session. Any plans must be dictated by the helpee's world and its possibilities and limits. It is not enough to talk about a variety of plans. Rather, specific consideration of the "hows" of the plans must occur. Planning for this helpee to meet new men at work will not succeed if very few men work with her; an alternative location needs to be sought.

8. *Arrange support for changes.* Increasing support for a helpee such as ours would be very useful by giving her someone with whom to discuss her plans. This other person could also provide praise as the helpee progressed through her plan. It could be a close friend who has been a good listener in the past and who would also be helpful in creating a good plan.

GENERAL BEHAVIOR CHANGE METHODS

With these general strategies in mind, the helper can design specific plans with the helpee's input and agreement. There are several general behavior change processes that the helper can consider, all of them alternatives for promoting change in helpees. Different processes are appropriate for different problems; four widely used methods are presented here.

Rehearsal

The helpee should try out the new behavior with the helper. If, for example, the goal is to become more assertive, the helpee should first practice this with the helper; or, if the helpee is to become more complimentary, this can also be practiced with the helper. This rehearsal or practice gives the helpee a chance to attempt the new behavior under optimal conditions. The helpee will be able to be certain of being able to perform as desired before attempting to do this in the natural environment.

Usually, the helper must be active in setting up a rehearsal experience, which typically takes the form of demonstrating or modeling the behavior for the helpee. Using role-playing, the helper shows the helpee what to do. The helper plays the role of the helpee in a simulation of a real-life situation and the helpee can enact the role of an important other person. In modeling, the helper not only demonstrates the behavior, but also describes it in detail before demonstrating and checks with the helpee after the demonstration to be sure the helpee has understood.

With one helpee, for example, one of the authors suggested learning how to give personal messages rather than make cutting remarks when something disturbed or angered him. The helper first defined personal messages for the helpee "as a statement of feelings about a particular behavior or situation with the feelings identified very clearly as your own." The helper then gave several examples: "I am very upset at what happened between us this morning. I feel bad because I didn't mean to usurp your turf, but I thought I was being helpful by making the meal. It was very upsetting to me when you yelled at me for doing that, and I found myself feeling angry at you, too." Following this, the helper suggested that the helpee construct personal messages to several stimulus statements made by the helper: for example, "Your wife parks the car in the street after you requested that she park it in the driveway." The helpee responded, "I'm very angry at you for parking the car in the street again." The helper and helpee examined this message and determined that it was a good beginning. At the same time, the language was a trifle strong and might be more facilitative if it were toned down a bit: "I'm annoyed to see that you parked the car in the street after we agreed you'd park in the driveway." Then the helper took the role of the helpee himself, and asked the helpee to role-play his wife in a recent conflict. The helper modeled the use of personal messages in such an encounter. Lastly, the helper took the role of the helpee's wife and enacted the conflict he had already described. This time, however, the helpee was to role-play himself and use personal messages. He thus had the opportunity to rehearse the new behaviors in a safe context before trying them outside of the helping relationship.

Rehearsal can be covert or overt. In other words, the helpee can *imagine* practicing the behavior (covert) or can *actually practice* the behavior (overt). Usually, covert rehearsal is used if the helpee finds the new behavior *exceedingly* difficult. With one adolescent helpee, the helper found her too shy and reluctant to experiment with new assertive behaviors even with the helper. So the helper suggested she first think the statements to herself. The two of them discussed her feelings after she did so. This continued for two sessions. Following this, the helper asked the helpee to verbalize out loud *after* thinking to herself. This time, she was better able to do so. They continued to practice in this limited way until the helpee felt less squeamish about role-playing, and then the helper took the role of the helpee's mother and had the helpee rehearse her own assertive statements. (She did indeed follow through with her mother and was pleasantly surprised at the positive and interested reception she got.) It's important to remember that overt rehearsal is the goal, so that covert practice is best seen as one step toward the goal.

Relaxation

Helpees who are quite anxious can benefit greatly from being taught how to relax. This can be done in several ways, either by using deep muscle relaxation or by using pleasant, calming thoughts to induce relaxation (see Benson, 1975; Bernstein & Borkovec, 1973).

For example, an older man complained of tension and tightness in his chest while working; his physician told him he had no physical problem. While helper and helpee examined his work situation and habits to determine how he might be inducing additional stress for himself, they also agreed that progressive relaxation training could be beneficial. The helpee was taught the procedure first by listening to a taped set of instructions, then by responding to the helper while giving the instructions, and lastly by responding to his own internal voice giving the instructions, first in the helper's office and then at home and work. The helper suggested, too, that the helpee think of the most relaxing image possible for him and visualize this during the relaxation process, particularly after all the stages had been gone through. The helpee did so, and reported an extra sensation of relaxation. He found himself calmer at work and at home as the relaxation training progressed. Complemented by several other changes in work behavior, the helpee reported complete cessation of chest tightness and of generalized tension.

While relaxation may help many people become more calm, it can be paired with other techniques for specialized problems. One procedure used very frequently is called systematic desensitization. This entails relaxation paired with imagined scenes that the helpee finds anxiety producing. These scenes are graded from low- to high-anxiety producing and are presented in order starting with the least anxiety producing to a relaxed helpee. In this way, the bond between the scene and the anxiety response is decreased.

A woman helpee complained of anxiety at public speaking. She identified several different situations, and noted that she didn't feel equally anxious in all of them. The helper suggested that they rank order the situations from least to most anxiety producing. They proceeded to tackle the relaxation procedure, following which the helper verbally paired each image with the relaxed state of the helpee. This was done one at a time, from least to most tension associated with the image, until the helpee reported no sensations of anxiety at all with any of the images. The process occurred over several sessions. Both agreed that a real-life test of the helpee's changed feelings would be useful. The helpee decided to volunteer first for a situation that used to produce middle-level anxiety. She did so well that she next volunteered for a high-level situation. She reported feeling an initial pang of anxiety, but it quickly disappeared and she was able to carry out the speaking role fluently and without difficulties. It must be noted that systematic desensitization is a specialized procedure requiring specific training. It should not be attempted without such training and supervision.

Restructuring of Thoughts

Helpees' ways of thinking can be at the root of their concerns, and it may help to deal with them directly. One's belief system may lead to unrealistic expectations or hopes. For example, many helpees believe the following irrational thoughts.[2]

1. You must—yes, *must*—have sincere love and approval almost all the time from all the people you find significant.
2. You must prove yourself thoroughly competent, adequate, and achieving; or you must at least have real competence or talent at something important.
3. People who harm you or commit misdeeds rate as generally bad, wicked, or villainous individuals; you should severely blame, damn, and punish them for their sins.

[2]From the book *A New Guide to Rational Living*, by Ellis and Harper.©1975 by Institute for Rational Living, Inc. Published by Prentice-Hall, Inc., Englewood Cliffs, New Jersey 07632.

4. Life proves awful, terrible, horrible, or catastrophic when things do not go the way you would like them to go.
5. Emotional misery comes from external pressures, and you have little ability to control your feelings or rid yourself of depression and hostility.
6. If something seems dangerous or fearsome, you must become terribly occupied with and upset about it.
7. You will find it easier to avoid facing many of life's difficulties and self-responsibilities than to undertake more rewarding forms of self-discipline.
8. Your past remains all-important; because something once strongly influenced your life, it has to keep determining your feelings and behavior today.
9. People and things should turn out better than they do; you have to view it as awful and horrible if you do not quickly find good solutions to life's hassles.
10. You can achieve happiness by inertia and inaction or by passively and uncommittedly "enjoying yourself."
11. You must have a high degree of order or certainty to feel comfortable; you need some supernatural power on which to rely.
12. You can give yourself a global rating as a human; your general worth and self-acceptance depend upon the goodness of your performances and the degree to which people approve of you.

Helpees actually say these things to themselves in life situations and thereby cause themselves great distress. The helper can discuss these thoughts and try to modify them. To do so, it's necessary for the helper to point them out to the helpee, note how they lead to problems, and work with the helpee to develop more constructive ways of thinking.

One of the authors, for instance, noted that a helpee was approaching weight control with one or two of these beliefs in operation. She seemed in particular to be telling herself that it was easier to avoid facing this difficulty than to attempt to master a rewarding form of self-discipline—changes in her eating habits. The helper made this observation, noting several specific behaviors and statements the helpee had made. The helpee was surprised, saying that she had not thought of it that way before. As they further explored, it became apparent that she told this to herself in many other situations and so did not accomplish any of the changes she purported to want. In other words, she set herself up for failure by ignoring certain difficulties and by giving up before she began. With specific reference to her eating habits, it became clear that the helpee made other self-statements that defeated her. For example, if she ate one cookie not on her program, she said to herself

"I've blown it now. I might as well finish the box." Her viewpoint was catastrophic, and her consequent behaviors self-defeating. By identifying her problematic self-statements through exploration and record keeping, helper and helpee were able to decrease them and to substitute more constructive thoughts: for example, "Although I ate this extra cookie, I'm still doing okay. I can stick to my program for the rest of the day." The helpee, over a period of time, was assisted not only in modifying her eating habits but also in being aware of what she told herself and how these statements affected her behaviors. She was taught how to gain control over her defeating behaviors.

Restructuring thoughts may involve less specific beliefs than those above. Parents of a 2-year-old girl were having difficulties weaning the child from the bottle. The girl's pediatrician had told them it was imperative that she stop drinking through nipples. Over a six-month period, different methods were attempted, such as offering the drink in a special mug with a ceramic animal at the bottom visible only when the cup was emptied. None had yet been effective. During discussions, exploration of thoughts and feelings of the parents occurred. It became evident that one parent believed that the child's loss of the sucking outlet was potentially psychologically damaging. She felt worried and sad, feeling a loss *for the child*. In reality, the loss was hers—the loss of her "baby." More concretely, she feared losing the cuddling time with her child, for bottles and cuddles went together. Her husband also worried about this, since he enjoyed the cuddling times as well. They were helped to rethink the situation and to tell themselves different "truths." For instance, "I can still cuddle with my child. I can create other opportunities; we can read stories and she can sit in my lap and hug. I will enjoy that immensely." Another belief that was encouraged was that the child would be likely to seek out additional cuddling times. Further, they were encouraged to tell themselves "My child will love me as much as before, even without my giving her the bottle." Coinciding with thought change, the parents decided to offer the bottle without any nipple, but with a straw. Since both parents felt more comfortable with the shift, there was greater chance for success. No mixed messages were given to the child. This was indeed effective; the child easily made the switch, cuddling did not cease, and other opportunities for cuddling were effected.

Reinforcement Planning

New behaviors are in need of reward or reinforcement to keep them in operation. The helper must help the helpee find ways to obtain such rewards. Significant others often can help—for instance, they may be asked to praise the helpee for trying new behavior—and the helpee also can give himself or herself rewards for trying out new behaviors. Many helpers work to determine what rewards the helpee would find appealing. Whether it be to give oneself 25¢ for each attempt or to allow oneself an appealing activity (making a long-distance call to a friend) is dependent on what each individual helpee values.

With the child having tantrums, the parents were taught how to extinguish the tantrum behaviors and how to reinforce more desirable behaviors. The plan included letting the child clearly know what the house rules were ("No cookies except with your milk before bedtime") and having the parents convey their expectations ("Both of us would like you to listen to the house rule. We do not want to see you argue or insist on having a cookie. We want you to understand that neither of us will give you one, except at night with your milk"). The parents were instructed to ignore the child's pleas and physical behaviors, occupying themselves with other tasks after they had repeated the house rule once for the boy. They were *not* to give him a cookie. Once he ceased his tantrum, they were to go to him and hug him, telling him they were pleased to see him more calm and suggesting an activity for both (or all three) to become involved in. They were to praise him for his willingness to participate in the activity and tell him how much they enjoyed playing with him. Thus, they were to provide social reinforcement for more desirable behaviors.

These four behavior change processes have wide applicability to helping situations. Each is considerably more complicated than these brief discussions suggest. We suggest you refer to the Suggested Readings to become more knowledgeable about them and other approaches.

The helper should remember that planning is difficult. A capable helper becomes familiar with a variety of helping strategies and behavior change methods. Specific plans using these are then developed with the helpee. Any plan could include several specific behavior change methods. In helping a reluctant woman confront a domineering father, a helper could suggest the helpee practice such confrontations with the helper and could also teach the helpee to believe that she *can* be successful. That way, in addition to learning assertive behaviors the helpee will gain self-confidence. The plan may go through several changes (following evaluation) before the most effective set of actions is reached.

EVALUATION

Given the complexity of planning, it comes as little surprise that many helpers give little attention to evaluating their work. Furthermore, most people find evaluation very threatening; after all, one may be shown to be failing. However, this is a counterproductive way to view evaluation in helping. Change can occur only under the right conditions, and there is no magical way for a helper to know what these conditions might be. Of course, with experience and skill, helpers become more proficient at gauging the likelihood of success of plans. But even the most experienced helper is always engaging in trial-and-error. Helping is simply not the kind of enterprise in which great precision is now possible. The evaluation issue is not "Have I failed as a helper?" but "Has the specific plan my helpee tried actually helped to attain the goals?" If not, another plan must be constructed. Evaluation is a part of helping and should be a continual process.

To do an evaluation of the success of plans, it is necessary to consider what information about success would be important. For example, information must be unbiased and objective to make a sound conclusion of success or failure. You as a helper might be certain that the plan worked, but you are probably too involved with the helpee's situation to make an unbiased judgment. The helpee's own observation or self-report is another source of information that may be biased. Perhaps somewhat less biased might be the reports of other people who are in the position to observe the helpee. Both significant others (like family members) and people with whom the helper has close contact (like co-workers) can provide more reliable information, or at least additional information, with which to assess progress and change. It might also be worthwhile to set up a behavioral "test" for the helpee in the natural environment, with the helper observing. You might observe the helpee talking to a difficult friend. You might watch a child to see if she has indeed given up drinking from a bottle. This might be the most objective way of evaluating your plan, though it is probably the most difficult to arrange.

The most reasonable solution to the question of how to evaluate plans is to obtain *different perspectives* on their outcomes. All of the information above is important, despite whatever biases might be included. Remember, however, that some objective evidence is really necessary. The helper and the helpee can discuss how this evidence could be obtained. A useful rule is to have information from the helpee, information from others, and some objective information that has been gathered in an unbiased way. A couple completing marital counseling can be asked about their current marital satisfaction; their counselor can give his or her perspective on their progress; and finally they can be observed discussing a conflict together. If both the couple and the counselor see success, the couple's style of conflict management should indeed be different from their initial approach.

SUMMARY

Effective helping is more than proficient use of verbal and non-verbal skills. A good "recipe" for helping also calls for the careful use of skills in planning change. Effective helping, then, might be defined as the directed use of helping skills for the full assessment of the helpee's situation to describe and understand the problem(s), the planning of change efforts that will allow the helpee to achieve his or her goals, and the evaluation of these efforts. Specific techniques are, of course, necessary for this process, but it is important for helpers to maintain a flexible approach to planning for change. The tools helpers have are not only techniques, but *problem-solving strategies* that can be applied to a broad set of helpee problems. No tool or strategy is a panacea but, in combination with sensitive listening and understanding, helpees can begin the process of change.

THOUGHT QUESTIONS

1. What makes assessing helpees' concerns difficult?
2. How would you assess the situation of a helpee who did not wish to talk with you?
3. What makes a behavior a "problem?"
4. Give an example of a behavior that society considers problematic but you don't.
5. How do helper values and needs enter into helping strategies?
6. How are nonverbal behaviors involved in helping strategies?
7. Give several examples of goal statements.
8. What are some ways a helper can provide support for helpee change?
9. When might you use rehearsal as a method? relaxation? thought restructuring? reinforcement planning?
10. Why would evaluating your helping be hard?

8

The Ethics of Helping

A drug counselor working with a young man forcefully discourages him from trying a new drug his friends have given him. The counselor, an ex-drug abuser himself, believes that drug use is wrong—that it's an escape. He tells this to the helpee in no uncertain terms.

A young woman tells her helper that she's pregnant and wants an abortion. The counselor thinks abortions are immoral. In discussing options, the helper dwells mainly on the negative aspects of abortion, although she says nothing about what her helpee *ought* to do. When the client leaves, the counselor feels she has done her duty by allowing her helpee to "make her own decision."

An urban police officer is called for duty at a high school undergoing racial conflict related to a new busing plan. Although he's supposed to represent the law—and the law has called for busing—he's personally opposed to it. He feels he should ignore his own attitudes, but he wonders if he can really be impartial. He doesn't think he has the right to his own opinions while on the job.

A counselor who works with battered wives is appalled by the beating her client has just received. Much of her body has been bruised and her jaw was broken. Losing her composure, the counselor recommends that the client have her husband arrested immediately, saying that she should not tolerate such treatment. The client, crying uncontrollably, reluctantly agrees, and the police are called.

Helpers are constantly surrounded with questions of right and wrong. Is it right to use drugs? Are abortions right? Is busing right? Is spouse abuse right? All of the helpers above might prefer to remain uninvolved with such questions, but they cannot. It is much easier to say that these are helpees' decisions than it is to remain honestly neutral in the face of mistreatment, injustice, and misery. The helpers above were engaged in making moral judgments—in deciding what was "right" or "moral" in these situations. They were bringing their personal views of morality—of what is right, valuable, good, ethical—into their helping relationships. As with helpers' needs, helpers' ethics can facilitate or hinder their helping relationships. It is extremely helpful to work with helpees to consider their feelings about the rightness and wrongness of life decisions, but it is certainly *not* helpful to make these decisions for them.

There is an important difference between helpers' needs and their ethics. A helper's needs are quite personal; each helper's unique development has resulted in his or her present needs. Ethics, however, are *shared*. A helper's judgments about right and wrong reflect the values and judgments of society in general and particularly the values of the organization for which he or she works. To explore helping ethics, one must carefully consider how one comes to a decision about right and wrong. One must also then scrutinize how ethics are involved in the daily routine of helping others. Helpers cannot leave their moral judgments out of helping any more than they can ignore their needs and motivations; nor can they avoid carrying their agencies' values into helping interactions.

This chapter will consider several ways in which morality and ethics are involved in helping. Helpers make judgments about the morality of their helpees' situations and they also judge their helpees' goals. Is seeking a divorce right? Is placing an aging parent in a nursing home right? We will start by discussing how morality can influence helping goals.

MORALITY AND HELPING GOALS

Morality always involves a choice. In making a decision about whether something is right or wrong, we use our personal standards of rightness and wrongness. These standards develop with us as we grow and experience life; they reflect our family, our community, and our society. Thus, morality is *personal* and yet is also *shared* with others. Our own standards may be consistent with those of some and radically different from those of others. You may have grown up in a family in which divorce was considered wrong, while another's family may be much more positive about divorce. Morality is, then, *relative*: there is no absolute "right" or "wrong" that is beyond debate. A final characteristic of morality is that it involves strong *emotions*. We often react very strongly to occurrences that we consider immoral. Child abuse is an example of the kind of problem that helpers generally consider "wrong" and react very emotionally to.

Since morality is so essential to our lives, we cannot simply put it aside when helping others. After all, helping is itself "good" in the moral sense. In other words, the most general assumption of helping—a basic belief in the ability of one person to aid another—is very worthwhile. Behind this value is a general belief in the goodness of people, in the worth of human beings. At its most basic, helping is the sharing of oneself with others to help them meet their needs. This is a general goal of helping that most agree is highly moral.

Another essential belief characterizes helping. This is the belief that people can be helped to change, improve, and enhance their daily lives. This belief in the possibility of *enhancement* is not necessarily coincident with a belief in the innate goodness of people, although it may often be related. Belief in the goodness, evil, or neutrality of human beings is a more general value. An effective helper may hold any one of those three positions if the helper also believes and works toward enhancing the lives of others. Without the affirmation of the possibility of *change*, the helper is helpless. Indeed, a person who does not believe change is possible may be acting immorally in becoming a helper, for such a stance would negate the very possibility of help-giving.

Although the value of helping as promoting change is not controversial, more specific goals of helping are often very debatable. Helpers are continually pursuing one or more of the following with their helpees:

1. providing information
2. educating
3. self-actualizing
4. training for skills in living
5. promoting decision-making
6. promoting adjustment
7. facilitating recognition of environmental constraints and opportunities
8. being supportive
9. teaching how to cope
10. raising awareness
11. clarifying values
12. remediating specific problems (speech difficulties, learning disabilities, and so on)

These goals are all positively oriented, well meaning, and indeed potentially helpful. The *intentions* of helpers pursuing these goals are honorable. Who can argue with the good intentions implied in the statement that helping, for example, is directed toward helping people find meaning and satisfaction in life?

However, consider "promoting adjustment" as a helping goal. Viewing the *effects* of helping has led some observers to conclude that help-giving, while well-intended, can be a major source of control over people. The consequences of help-giving may be to hold people in line, to promote conformity to "the party line" of the larger society in the guise of helping people to resolve difficulties in living. This can be seen in the goal of helping people become "well-adjusted."

A key to this moral dilemma in helping is the focus on the source or "cause" of difficulties in living. Does the helping "blame" the victim or "blame" the environment? If the helper believes that the sole source of problems is the individual and that individual weaknesses and problems are the cause of the difficulties, the helper may be ignoring the evidence that social systems such as families, neighborhood or work groups, and communities have potent impact on individuals. If the helper views all problems in living as stemming solely from environmental oppression, the helper is ignoring the fact that individuals make up the system and do indeed have very real problems, or at least can—like systems—always be improved.

The Influence of Social Systems

But the issue is even more fundamental than that. It has to do with the helper's orientation to an *adjustment model* of helping vs. an *enhancement model*. It also has to do with the helper's willingness and ability to intervene in *systems* as well as to work with *individuals*. Social systems range from the small but psychologically significant— such as the family, neighborhood, peer groups, school classes, and the school itself—to larger systems like the local community, the state, and the nation. Intangible systems exist, too—such as the institutions of education, criminal justice, the family, and so on. Often it is the case that a helper who is adjustment-oriented is unwilling and/or unknowledgeable about how to change or enrich systems. The significance of these issues for this chapter lies in the power of the system to encourage the use of helping for social control, even when the helper *is* aware of the differences between adjustment and enhancement.

Helpers and helpees have been socialized within the same basic system, but, unlike helpees, helpers are employees of the system. All systems once established tend to act so as to maintain themselves and the general status quo. Helpers, as noted earlier, are constrained to engage in certain helping policies—if not in specific helping behaviors— by their agencies, whether they be schools, universities, community mental health centers, hospitals, police departments, or other public or private agencies. Many policies are *unwritten*; that is, they exist within agencies but are informally communicated as expectations. For instance, school counselors rarely know of a specific policy regarding abortion counseling, but often feel that either the topic should be avoided or that the school and community expect the counselor to advise against it. Other examples abound, particularly those regarding similar controversial social issues like racism, sexism, drug use/abuse, homosexual behavior, and sexual conduct.

Social control, then, may be explicit as in a given agency's formal policies regarding certain aspects of helping. Most often, it is implicit and is manifested in unwritten policies. Social control is the *imposition of values*. In our example concerning abortion, we referred to the imposition of values through unwritten system policies. However, the larger system in this case—the nation—has agreed that, *legally*, abortions are to be a personal decision. The school, then, clearly ought to uphold the law of the land in spirit as well as letter: all counselors in the school should be encouraged to deal forthrightly with the issue in terms of the nation's laws. The actions of the system—permitting contrary policies and putting pressure on helpers to conform—are immoral. What of the actions of particular counselors within the system? If a helper *personally* condemns abortion, does the helper have the right to impose that position on helpees? Or is the helper obligated to inform the helpee of abortion as an alternative?

Adjustment versus Enhancement within Systems

More subtle social control is exerted in general help-giving when no particular socially controversial issue is directly involved. Again, this concerns emphasizing *adjustment* in the individual vs. *enhancement* for individuals and systems. Most helpers see their mission as alleviating emotional or physical suffering and unhappiness. As noted earlier, helping behaviors toward this end are guided by a particular belief system that involves some view of the sort of changes that will improve helpees' lives. Traditionally, helpers have been trained to think in terms of individual change. Most typically, this change is regarded as being necessitated by the individual's inability to adjust adequately to the social world or the "system." Many helpers conceptualize their helping goals under the umbrella concept of "teaching good coping skills."

Coping suggests adjustment to present social conditions. For this reason, some helpers have called this type of helping unethical. This criticism has been raised for two reasons. First, many people become helpees because social judgment has indicated or demanded that they receive help in improving their adjustment to society. Their behaviors are judged to be *unreasonable,* whether the label is "emotionally disturbed," "retarded," "criminal," "ignorant," or "sick." The judgments, often made voluntarily by the helpee, are based upon what Halleck (1971) asserts are shifting, if not arbitrary, criteria to which participants in the system become socialized. The value judgments lie in the facts that (1) not every participant agrees with the conventional, often stereotyped or conformity-based, criteria and (2) "normal" behavior is simply that—average—and most social values stress average behavior. Any other behaviors, however creative or unusual, are *deviant*. Deviance is socially defined often for the convenience of the majority or of those in power. Helpers often engage in fostering conformity under the guise of "adjustment."

The second reason is that those helpers who participate in helping by encouraging adjustment to the current system are to a large extent giving *legitimacy* to the system (Halleck, 1971). By acting in accord with the openly acknowledged goal of fostering individual conformity, the helper provides credibility to what may be unviable or indeed immoral systems. Acting on behalf of any system implies that the system is worthy of respect, attention, and perhaps even obedience. Helping based on individual adjustment is pragmatic in the short term: it makes the current situation more tolerable and perhaps acceptable for the individual. It also makes it more comfortable for the system. No challenge is made and the system may continue as is. But such helping is questionable, since it leaves institutions in need of change essentially unchanged.

Other helpers call for positive actions to do away with unethical social control by helpers. These helpers call for *activist* helping largely concerned with challenging social systems and encouraging individuals to actively engage in confronting oppressive systems.

At its broadest, some people assert that helpers must counsel actively for peace instead of war. They argue that the real helpees are not those so identified by society, but rather the social institutions themselves, such as sexism and racism. The helping behaviors they encourage concern assisting the individual to develop skills to challenge the system. Both helpers and helpees should do such things as speaking out against the explicit and implicit oppressive policies, working toward reform of laws, and recognizing careers that stress peace and welfare. Helpers must confront helpees (and others) regarding racist and sexist attitudes, indeed, must confront others regarding any discriminatory and divisive attitudes and behaviors.

A similar but more extensive belief is held by Dworkin and Dworkin (1971). Their basic premise is that fitting people into existing systems manifests "help-destroyers, not help-givers" (p. 749). They assert that a helper may choose to either sit on the sidelines *or* have an impact on the direction and means of change. They point out various alternative helping behaviors that can ameliorate social problems. For example, they recognize an emerging trend to repression of civil liberties. Their suggested help-giving behaviors include becoming informed about recent legislation and court decisions, helping to organize free legal aid clinics, intervening on behalf of helpees when their civil liberties have been denied, and helping helpees to organize themselves to assert their rights. Regarding the search for alternatives to traditional and sexist careers, the Dworkins suggest that the helper acquire relevant information and make it available to helpees, help people involve themselves in social-action vocations, help people to develop skills as active participants in social change, and help in establishing community-based day care, medical, and legal aid centers, and inform helpees of *true* working conditions in different settings.

Various helpers, then, maintain that moral help-giving involves more than making an individual's life situation more tolerable. The helper is to take action to assist helpees in developing power to direct change in their own lives and social systems. In this way, both individuals and systems will benefit. When the powerless—those labeled deviant or in the minority—learn and begin to take action for themselves, they affect their existence and destiny. Their horizons expand and their beliefs about themselves and actions toward others are altered. Their action also effects major changes in the response of others to the individual in the smaller social systems—the class, the school, the family, the job setting—and can effect changes in the larger system, primarily because the individual will be willing to make necessary confrontations. The helper not only must assist the individual in actively adjusting to the system, but also must help the system to adjust to the needs of the helpee.

We caution those helpers who seek to be helpful by asserting activist values and behaviors in helping relationships. Such an orientation does not justify imposing values on helpees. "Laying a trip" on helpees will prove counterproductive and threatening. Rather, the helper helps by redefining the situation, reframing the identified problems in different ways, working toward specified enhancement goals rather than toward a general goal of "adjustment," becoming involved in relevant challenges to the system, and so on—a quiet but active helping revolution.

Evolving Your Own View of Moral Help-Giving

The means by which a helper prepares to engage in moral help-giving is through examination of his or her own values in living and helping. To evaluate forces of social change with open minds, helpers must reassess their own life styles. They must evaluate their attitudes and beliefs about all aspects of their lives, including leisure time pursuits, books and magazines, the organizations and groups that attract them, and so on. The helper must engage in personal consciousness-raising too. For example, a well-intentioned but sexist counselor will do harm to both female and male clients. Such a counselor will not only channel female clients into traditional and sexist roles and attitudes if not actual careers, but will also perpetuate such attitudes (and roles) in male clients. Even alert counselors succumb inadvertently to some sexist orientations. Whether the issue is sexism, racism, or other discriminatory attitudes, the moral helper in any role has to do more than be aware that such attitudes exist. The helper must actively confront his or her personal assumptions and actual behaviors and must take steps to change them if necessary. Self-change, in life style and attitudes, involves some risk-taking. It is difficult and frustrating but, just as helpers encourage helpees to enhance their skills in living, they must do so themselves. Further, their moral responsibilities as helpers require lifelong vigilance and activity in this regard. Self-change and social change are *processes,* not events.

Through self-examination and self-change processes, the helper will evolve a view of moral help-giving. The helper clarifies personal needs and values not only to make the orientation explicit to helpees as appropriate, but also to free the helpee from them. This is social freedom, not social control.

As Halleck (1971) notes, every helper has some notion regarding the best kind of life for each helpee. Furthermore, every helpee who has benefitted from helping has incorporated some of the helper's values. This is the reality that cannot be avoided. It *can* be confronted constructively. The helper's moral responsibilities are to respect and care for helpees' welfare above all. Doing so requires personal and professional values clarification, examination of agency and institutional policies and practices, and involvement in social change processes. Respecting the confidentiality of a helpee's disclosures, advising the helpee of any limits to that confidentiality, discussing the helping "contract" and arriving at a mutually agreeable definition, and maintaining standards of competence and performance are parts of the helper's ethical obligations. These must be based on the helper's own personal ethical awareness and integrity. Not only must the helper be a caring and alert social critic (Halleck, 1971), but she or he also must be an honest and persevering personal critic.

We have raised many questions and have answered few. Morality is largely personal. At the same time, the ethics of the helping professions must be adhered to, as helpers have a social contract to do so. The helper's job is to fit the two together into a code for helping and living—a code where the behaviors, intentions, and effects are consistent and meaningful.

In helping others, you communicate your own feelings as well as listen for the helpees' feelings. Helpers do this both *inadvertently,* through nonverbal cues, and *deliberately,* through self-involving. In assisting helpees to set goals for themselves, whether these goals involve self-change or systems change, helpers cannot help but draw on their own experiences in living. This is *human* helping behavior. People draw on their past, their present, and their hopes and ambitions for the future when they interact with others. We are unique in that we remember earlier experiences in later contexts. However, helpers traditionally have been told to avoid discussing their own experiences with helpees and, in fact, to disclose very little about themselves. This was to permit the greatest amount of attention to the helpees' concerns and to strategies for dealing with them. It is obvious that the more a helper discloses, the less chance the helpee will have to do so. The moral goal in this stance has to do with avoiding the imposition of helper values on helpees. Does a helper have the right to communicate his or her own personal point of view on an issue?

Traditionally, the response to this question has been "no." The conventional wisdom has been that helpers must not speak about or indicate their own values in living or their viewpoints on any particular sensitive issues. The helper was supposed to remain a "blank wall." As we've said in other chapters, there is now widespread recognition that (1) helpers communicate values and opinions by subtle behavioral cues, (2) helper responses are influenced by personal values and affect helpee views and behavior, and (3) the goals of helping for a specific helper may well be very much influenced by his or her values in living. Therefore, the question now becomes: *How* can the helper convey her or his own values in ways that will prove *constructive* to the helping process?

The moral issue is recognizing the values implicit in helping and making them explicit. One reason for the stress on making values explicit is that by doing so, the helper gives the helpee freedom of choice to remain in or withdraw from a particular helping relationship. If the values are compatible, the helpee will choose to remain and is more likely to work toward agreeable and constructive goals. If the helper's values are inconsistent with those of the helpee, the option of disengaging from that relationship provides an opportunity to seek out a more compatible helper. Therefore, the moral approach to helping gives the helpee information upon which to make a decision about "contracting" for help.

Perhaps the first step toward achieving morality in helping goals is for the helper to examine thoroughly his or her own values and goals in living and in helping. Awareness of your needs in helping permits greater control over their influences on your helping behavior; awareness of your values and personal goals facilitates constructive control over their influences in the helping context. Secondary benefits of such self-exploration may be in clarifying your own values and redefining your personal goals and life style.

One helper has shared his experiences in confronting personal values in living and helping. He found that his values most definitely entered into his perspective on help-giving and into his helping relationships. This became particularly clear when he began to work with urban teenagers, a group that had distinctly different values, goals, *and* living experiences from his own.

> As my extensive work with teenagers has continued over the years, I have had to come to grips with some of the most basic questions concerning myself as a person. I have had to re-evaluate my analytic training and therapeutic practices as I apply them in practice. My value system has come under self-scrutiny. The reflections and shifts have made a real impact upon me both as a human being and as a psychoanalyst.... I do not believe that an analyst can work with the dissenting youth of today if he continues to hide behind the old dictum of "I reflect the problems of my patients; my own values do not enter in." They intrude from the moment a young person enters my office [Freudenberger, 1971, p. 38].

This helper chose, after examining his values in helping and living, to change his life style to some degree. He changed his leisure pursuits from reading abstract treatises to reading counter-culture literature. Further, he began to wander around the clinic's neighborhood, to learn the locale and the community, and to afford opportunities for him to chat with the young people of the area outside the context of his office and role. His goals were to learn more about people and a way of life he had not understood before, to take part in this way of life, and to develop a sense of trust between the people and himself. Lastly, he drastically modified his therapeutic strategies to fit better with the lives of these people and with his revised understanding of himself and his values.

A FRAMEWORK FOR ANALYZING HELPERS' MORAL DECISIONS

Recently, social scientists have found it useful to consider the processes by which people make decisions as to what is moral. What is the nature of the thinking that leads a helper, for example, to consider verbal abuse of a spouse as immoral? How does a child welfare agency decide that an alcoholic woman should not have custody of her child? On what basis does a society decide that birth control is morally acceptable? All of these hypothetical decisions are made by *moral reasoning,* defined as the process by which the morality of situations is evaluated.

Lawrence Kohlberg (1963, 1969, 1976) has developed a system for classifying different types of moral reasoning. In his view, individuals (and, by extension, agencies and societies, which are groups of individuals) differ in how they arrive at moral judgments. They process actions in distinctly different ways before calling the actions "moral" or "immoral." Kohlberg (1969, p. 376) proposes six types, or stages, of reasoning, as defined in Table 8-1.

Let us now consider how a helpee's problem can be evaluated from the perspective of the various moral judgment stages. The decision-making process is more important than the final decision itself of rightness or wrongness.

The Ethics of Helping 157

Table 8-1. Moral Reasoning Orientations.

Level I: Preconventional. Moral value resides in external, quasi-physical happenings, in bad acts, or in quasi-physical needs rather than in persons and standards.
   Stage 1: Obedience and Punishment. Egocentric deference to superior power or prestige, or a trouble-avoiding set. Objective responsibility.
   Stage 2: Instrumental Relativism. Right action is that which instrumentally satisfies the self's needs and occasionally others'. Awareness of relativism of value to each actor's needs and perspective. Naive egalitarianism and orientation to exchange and reciprocity.

Level II: Conventional. Moral value resides in performing good or right roles, in maintaining the conventional order and the expectations of others.
   Stage 3: Personal Concordance. Good-boy/good-girl orientation. Orientation to approval and to pleasing and helping others. Conformity to stereotypical images of majority or natural role behavior, and judgment by intentions.
   Stage 4: Law and Order. Orientation to "doing duty" and to showing respect for authority and maintaining the given social order for its own sake. Regard for earned expectations of others.

Level III: Postconventional. Moral value resides in conformity by the self to shared or shareable standards, rights, or duties.
   Stage 5A: Social Contract. Recognition of an arbitrary element or starting point in rules or expectations for the sake of agreement. Duty defined in terms of contract, general avoidance of violation of the will or rights of others, and majority will and welfare.
   Stage 5B (formerly 6): Individual Principles. Orientation not only to actually ordained social rules but to principles of choice involving appeal to logical universality and consistency. Orientation to conscience as a directing agent and to mutual respect and trust.

Stages of Moral Development © 1958 by Lawrence Kohlberg. Adapted from "Stage and Sequence: The Cognitive-Developmental Approach to Socialization," by L. Kohlberg. In D. Goslin (Ed.), *Handbook of Socialization Theory and Research.* Chicago: Rand McNally, 1969.

Let us assume a helpee is discussing with a helper an extramarital relationship. Let us also assume the helper finally judges the behavior "moral." How might the *helper* have arrived at this decision? If you could listen in to the helper's thoughts, what would you hear?

Stage	*Possible Helper Reasoning*
Obedience and punishment	"Helpee didn't get caught, so it's OK; no one found the helpee 'in the act,' so it's moral."
Instrumental relativism	"Helpee needed a different sexual outlet since she/he is having marital problems. Her/his needs were met and no one was really hurt."

Personal concordance	"A lot of adults have extramarital sex. Nothing's wrong with that. They're still good people."
Law and order	"Helpee was doing what her/his relationship called for. She/he feels they are responsible, mature people and are willing to accept the consequences."
Social contract	"Helpee and spouse have agreed that occasional affairs are OK. This agreement was mutual; both knew what they were agreeing to."
Universal principles	"Helpee seems to genuinely care about both spouse and lover. Helpee has taken into account their respective feelings and reactions. That helpee has cared so much about the consequences of her/his behavior that this makes her/his actions morally OK."

An example of a *helpee's* various ways of judging the morality of her own behavior follows. The helpee is contemplating an abortion. Let's assume the helpee has decided that abortion is wrong for her.

Stage	Possible Helpee Reasoning
Obedience and punishment	"I could get caught. My husband could find out and might want to divorce me."
Instrumental relativism	"I really can support the baby. I'm just being selfish, not wanting to be inconvenienced."
Personal concordance	"A good mother could never kill a baby like this. It's not natural."
Law and order	"The commandment says 'Thou shalt not kill.' I must follow that rule."
Social contract	"Society is changing its mind in favor of abortion, but I must still follow my own personal views. A lot of people look at it differently, but I must live with my own decision."
Universal principles	"Taking life away is morally wrong. I know it's just the 'possibility' of life at this point, but it's still alive. Under no circumstances would I want to deprive a living thing of life."

Finally, let's take an example of how an *agency* makes decisions about what's right or wrong for helpees. A drug treatment center prohibits the use of any drug (even cigarettes) on its premises. In this example, we're discussing the implicit reasoning at work, since most agencies do not act in a straightforward way as far as their moral decision-making is concerned.

Stage	*Possible Agency Reasoning*
Obedience and punishment	"We could get busted if we're caught with drugs in the building."
Instrumental relativism	"We want to look good in the neighborhood. We'll gain this reputation only if you drug users play it cool here."
Personal concordance	"How can any self-respecting drug center allow drug use? It would be ludicrous; we'd be so hypocritical."
Law and order	"State laws are very clear about illicit drugs. We have our own laws about other drugs and you should obey them. It's for the good of the center."
Social contract	"As a group, we have in the past agreed upon these rules. They protect all of us. You'll have to follow them because they represent our group's consensus and you have agreed to live with our rules."
Universal principles	"We want to protect people here and we're going to try as hard as we can to arrange the environment to be maximally helpful and not destructive."

As an exercise, go back to the very beginning of this chapter to the four situations presented. Consider how each helper came to a decision. Do this using each of the six different stages of moral reasoning.

MORALITY OF HELPING

This discussion of morality provides a framework for specifically considering the morality of helping. Evaluating the morality of a set of helper's behaviors must include a consideration of the *behaviors* themselves, the helper's *intentions,* and the actual *effects* of the behaviors on the helpee. Helping behaviors are often assumed to be inherently moral because they are viewed as altruistic, as the giving of aid and assistance to others with no strings attached. It is usual to consider altruism as unselfishness with no expectation of returns. Yet helping relationships satisfy certain needs of the helper whether they be needs for esteem, status, recognition, and so on as we've said earlier.

Given that helper needs are somehow met, it is obvious that in helping something is also *returned*. However, the returns are not the usual ones from interpersonal relationships, like the willingness to lend money or to provide transportation if a car breaks down. Other interpersonal returns—friendship outside of the helping sessions, physical intimacy, companionship at leisure events—are neither expected nor sought. There is no *quid pro quo* or instrumental relativist aspect to the helping relationship. The helper puts no interpersonal strings on the helpee. The intentions in helping are not to develop a friendship in the most usual sense of the term or to obligate the helpee to reciprocate interest. Rather, the returns that the helper expects are intangible. They are unrelated to the *specific* helper/helpee relationship but are expectations of need satisfaction from helping in general. The helper expects to feel important, to feel that the meeting was worthwhile, to feel that something was accomplished.

The Contract

A helper works to help others in ways that they and/or society specify, offering assistance of a specialized nature for determining and working toward particular goals. One defining aspect of helping relationships is that they are *contractual,* knowingly entered into by helpers and helpees for specific purposes. For most helping relationships, the contract is *implied.* This is particularly true in outpatient clinics, community mental health centers, and outreach services, because the helpees come *voluntarily.* The helper and helpee jointly determine how they will work together. They discuss the reasons for entering into a relationship and outline the general purposes of such a relationship. Such a helping relationship, guided by social contract reasoning, is a highly moral one: both parties have some say and both agree to its terms. Moreover, the helper allows the helpee the freedom of withdrawing from the relationship. The helper indeed should be willing to discuss personal values with the helpee, particularly values that might interfere with good listening. The helpee can be seen to be contracting for a service and can literally "take it or leave it."

Many helping relationships are not of this type, but are *involuntary*. Helpees are *expected* or *forced* to participate in helping relationships in some settings. For example, children in classrooms, prisoners seen by rehabilitation counselors, institutionalized mental patients, and medical patients in a hospital seldom have a real choice of helper or type of helping. The defining characteristic of these relationships is that the helper's employer is an *institution* in which the *helpees are legally present*: a school, a hospital, a prison. These employers are branches of the larger institutions organized by society to perform specific functions for the *good of society*. These institutions have been formed in the past through social contracts; that is, members of our society (at least in the past) have agreed to the need for the organization. There remains consensus that schools are essential, that prisons serve important functions, and that some mentally retarded people can benefit from institutional life. Although helpees receive a benefit from these institutions, society does as well. In any event, helpees have little choice but to be present in such places.

On the other hand, even though the helpee may have little choice, does that mean that helping offered is not "moral" or "good"? To put it concretely, does society have the right to help some of its members in a way *it* deems helpful? The way helpers answer this question, of course, will reflect their moral reasoning orientation. How would *you* answer this question?

Helpers and the Status Quo

Helpers in institutionalized helping roles may be seen as upholding the social order. Their roles imply maintenance of the system, as set forth at some earlier time by the larger society. Indeed, those hired in such helping positions are explicitly asked to follow certain system rules and to give certain kinds of help in specifically defined ways. Police, for example, may have highly individualized beliefs about busing and racial integration; given the law of the land, they are *required* to ensure that busing is carried out safely. Helping, therefore, is defined to a great extent by the particular policies of a particular agency or organization within the larger system. When helpers are hired by an agency, they are implicitly agreeing to work within the policy bounds of that agency. Nurses may be asked to assist in abortions at particular hospitals as a matter of policy, whereas others may permit individual choice in such instances. If a nurse judges abortion to be morally wrong, should this person be obligated as a helper to assist?

Following the policies of an agency simply because they are so stated would reflect a law-and-order orientation to morality. If the nurse personally feels that abortion is morally wrong but agrees to assist in abortions because others have a right to their own moral views and the larger society has legislated it, this nurse is oriented to the social contract involved. If despite differing views, the nurse agrees to assist because the laws of the land must be obeyed, the orientation is to law and order. If the nurse agrees to assist despite differing personal views because of a supervisor's expectation and approval, the moral orientation is personal concordance: judging and acting consistently with the expectations of the role. If the nurse agrees to assist despite differing personal views because doing so will ensure a promotion, the moral orientation is instrumental relativism: focusing on personal gain and what needs to be done to ensure it. If, despite differing personal views, the nurse agrees to assist only because not helping may result in being fired, the moral orientation is punishment avoidance. The point is that morality is not easy to define, nor is it clear in all instances. Moreover, people may make the *same decision* for *different moral reasons*. Morality in helping is no exception.

SUMMARY

Helpees' lives involve choices and decisions, as do all of our lives. In offering help, helpers are often drawn into moral decisions about helpees and their circumstances. The goals of a helper in working with a particular helpee may reflect the helper's moral decisions about what is a "good life." The helper may not be aware of how his or her moral decisions are entering the helping relationship. However, just as helpers must explore their needs, they must also carefully study their moral stances and their moral decision-making. We suggest that helpers can benefit from looking at their moral choices and how they arrive at these choices. Uninformed helpers may be imposing their own morality, whereas informed helpers can be honest with helpees about their values. This kind of personal honesty results in "moral helping" in which both helper and helpee are aware of the social contract they are forging.

THOUGHT QUESTIONS

1. Under what conditions is helping immoral?
2. Can a helpee be helped even if he or she is unwilling to ask for help?
3. On what issues do you hold strong value positions?
4. How would you work with a helpee from a very different background?
5. Give an example of a situation in which a helpee *should* adjust to social expectations.
6. Give an example of a situation in which a helpee *should not* adjust to social expectations.
7. Assume a helpee told you that he or she was about to harm a relative. What would you do? Would you contact the police?
8. Does a helpee have the right to commit suicide? Would you stop someone from taking his or her own life?
9. Would you consider your lifestyle as radical, moderate, or conservative? How will this intrude into your helping?
10. Would you become involved in social change efforts? Why or why not?

Epilogue: To Help or Not to Help

Imagine yourself as a helper. How do you see yourself? Where will you be helping? A private office, a storefront clinic, a rambly outreach center located in an old Victorian house, a preschool playroom, a school, a police station, a hospital ward, a neighbor's house? What kinds of helpees will you work with? Young children, troubled marital partners, families dealing with death, men confronting the boredom of prison life, older adults trying to avoid life in nursing homes? How effective will you be in helping? Will you be working with people for whom change is feasible or with those who see their lives as hopelessly out of their control? How will your skills meet the acid test of real helpees with real problems?

A great many unknowns confront the beginning helper. Many of these questions can only be answered with experience, since the answers depend on individual circumstances. However, the nature of helping others changes to some extent over time because of changing conditions that have little to do with an individual helper. We began the book by looking into the past, showing how the nature of helping reflects the times. Now let's look into the future of helping others. From the perspective of current helping patterns, what is likely in the future? How will people resolve pressing personal problems and further develop their lives? The answers to such questions will help resolve the issue of what personal helping will become. As this issue becomes clarified, you may find a sharper image of yourself as helper beginning to emerge.

THE NEED FOR HELPING

All available evidence points to the likelihood that there will be ever-increasing numbers of persons and families with problems; we already know that more problems exist than are ever resolved by our human services. It is also possible that our society will in the future place increasing stresses upon people. The economic situation alone may place undue burdens upon families to meet their basic needs. Many other societal forces are likely to cause problems, among them inflation, sexism, racism, and the dwindling resources in a country not accustomed to limits. As discussed in Chapters 1 and 7, many factors influence the development of problem behavior. If we expect social conditions to worsen, we can predict an increase in problems on an individual and family level.

As helpers, it is important that we not "blame the victim." Many social and economic forces that cause stress in individuals and families are certainly out of their control. A social worker counseling a helpee who is out of work might be tempted to attribute this situation to the person's lack of enthusiasm or to self-defeating attitudes. While it is possible that these problems contribute to the person's continued unemployment, the helper should be cautious to conclude that these factors *caused* the employment problem. Of course, the helper could still choose to work with this person in a variety of different ways, ranging from teaching the person assertiveness skills to referring the person to an employment service.

A second aspect of the future need for helping relates to our increased sensitivity to many kinds of human problems. For example, child abuse has only recently become a national concern, although abuse has existed for a long time. A problem once quietly discussed among neighbors of an abused child has attracted much attention, and much helping is currently targeted to dealing with such abuse. Individual parents are helped to overcome their abusing patterns of behavior through counseling, whether voluntary or court-ordered. Help is also offered through groups organized for abusing parents in which they can share their experiences and feelings and ways of constructively handling difficult situations with their children. Often parenting classes are held for such parents with the hope that they can prevent future abuse by learning new ways to deal with conflict.

In a similar way, we are now increasingly aware of the needs of the elderly. Many helping programs have been developed to enhance the physical and social well-being of the elderly, who were once the forgotten elders of social services. During the days of the settlement houses and the Charity Organization Societies, the elderly were in focus as warranting assistance. However, the rapid social changes in this century and shifting views and values regarding youth and aging generally pushed the elderly to the wayside. The needs of the elderly have, then, been "rediscovered" and many programs ranging from "Meals on Wheels," in which nutritious meals are brought to older people, to planned social activities are available.

A third example of the raising of our consciousness of problem situations has resulted from the women's movement. Women have become increasingly active in designing helping services for their own needs. Although many women have in the past been brutalized by their spouses, only recently have women sought special helping services for this problem. Similarly, the unique crisis that a rape victim undergoes has formed the basis for rape counseling, a helping service that results from the recently developed understanding of this special problem. A tremendous variety of services are now available that are exclusively oriented to women. In addition to rape counseling, for example, assertiveness groups, self-help groups, and rape prevention groups are provided in many communities.

A fourth major trend in the future of helping services is found in the recognition that many typical life events lead to problems for people and families. Changing jobs, having a baby, buying a home, moving to a new area, being promoted to a more demanding position, and retiring are all *typical* events—most of us will experience them. In addition, many of us will experience stress; for some of us, it will be crisis. These are events that most of us can expect, and we will deal with them either well or poorly, depending on our coping abilities at the time they occur. There are also more *unexpected* life events—such as sudden death, a separation, or a job loss—that take people by surprise. How we handle them depends on our psychological and social resources at the time. A sudden death is traumatic for anyone, but for some this leads to long-lasting life crisis and despair. Along with the recognition that life events, planned or unexpected, can be stressful, helping services have recently been designed to help people deal with these events more effectively, in preventive and enhancement senses. There are, for example, many classes to prepare expectant parents for childbirth and child care, both stressful for the unprepared. There are also programs designed to help widows deal with loneliness, programs to help executives manage stress and to rethink priorities related to family life, programs to assist neighbors in learning how to better listen to and help other community members, and so on.

The likelihood that social and economic conditions will continue to result in many personal problems, the increased awareness of problem areas that for a long time had not been given adequate attention, and the recognition that many common life events are stressful all lead to the same general conclusion: there will certainly be a need for personal helping experiences in the future. Indeed, it is likely that even more helpers will be needed.

WHO WILL HELP?

We noted in Chapter 1 that there are many kinds of helpers currently working with people. Partly because of financial factors and partly because of the expansion of views regarding who is able to help, many of these helpers are now nonprofessionals and paraprofessionals.

Compared to professional helpers, paraprofessionals and nonprofessionals have less academic experience, although they often have as much practical experience in helping. Paraprofessionals have received specialized training in helping and have a formal helping role of some sort, whereas nonprofessionals do not have such a formal role. The future of helping services will promote the increased use of nonprofessionals and paraprofessionals. This is not to say that professionals will no longer exist, nor is it to say that they will not provide leadership in the helping services. Indeed, they will. But the notion that "help" can come in many forms has received broad acceptance. As a matter of fact, what we are likely to see in the future is greater reliance on local community members for help and on self-help of one kind or another.

The deprofessionalization of helping has been occurring for many years. We have become aware, for example, that most people do not turn first to professionals for help with personal problems. People do not like to admit to problems, nor do they often know about the kinds of help available. For many people, admitting the need for help is tantamount to admitting failure. In addition, the process of locating help is often difficult. Urban areas often have an overwhelming, bewildering number of highly specialized professional helping services: which is suitable to what types of problems or goals? Rural areas often have very few services, and they are hard to reach. The often complex procedures followed to get help—scheduling appointments, filling out forms, undergoing "intake" interviews, and so forth—also make access to help more difficult. For these reasons, in addition to those noted in the beginning chapter, the future of helping does not lie so much with increased professional services as with services provided by other kinds of helpers.

Human services for helping will continue to exist in most communities, though funding is likely to be a perpetual problem. More and more of the helpers will be paraprofessionals and nonprofessionals. The "direct service" providers will have training in helping skills such as those we've described here, but they are unlikely to have the theoretical background or evaluation skills of the professional. These helpers are likely to be trained and supervised by the professional. In many cases, they will be local residents and therefore have the potential to relate more directly to the special concerns of fellow residents. Such indigenous helping, particularly if highly skilled, goes a long way in providing viable helping resources for people.

Another likely resource for the future by-passes trained helpers completely. This is the self-help area, one with a long history in the human services (Gartner & Riessman, 1977). Self-help occurs in many forms, ranging from reading a book on personal growth and self-acceptance to attending a group meeting of fellow alcoholics, drug abusers, or hypertensives. Both of these forms of self-help—reading books and attending groups—have become increasingly popular. Many books exhort people to be more positive about themselves; some provide specific suggestions for changing behavioral patterns. Similarly, some self-help groups are support groups, providing acceptance and caring for their members, while other groups encourage their members to act differently. An example of a support group is Parents Without Partners, an organization that provides a social context for discussion of renewed singlehood and its attendant problems and pressures. Alcoholics Anonymous is the most well-known example of a behavior-changing self-help group. The most basic commonality of all kinds of self-help is the lack of reliance on a formal helper, with great reliance on fellow helpers. Either the person alone or the person in a group of similar people is considered capable of change. Self-help is perhaps the logical extension of the deprofessionalization of helping services.

In sum, there will likely be many problems for helpers to deal with in the future. There will also be a range of helping resources available—professional, paraprofessional, nonprofessional, and self-help. However, since helping can have a facilitative, a destructive, or a neutral impact on helpees, it is critical that the type of help given is *skilled*.

THE FUTURE HELPER

It would not be surprising if this look into the future left you with this question: "How do I fit into all this?" You may have gotten the impression that there will be no place for the type of help we've described in this book. Will the movement toward deprofessionalization and self-help make the helper obsolete?

The answer to this question lies in the theme of this book—that helping is a skilled activity that must be learned. We think it is a myth that people are "naturally" helpful to each other, that spontaneous conversation between helper and helpee constitutes help, and that helpers need only good intentions and warmth to make a difference. Just as professional helping can at times be unhelpful, so may nonprofessionals, paraprofessionals, or self-helping be distinctly unhelpful. A community helper can misunderstand a helpee's concern; a helping neighbor can give demeaning advice; a support group can reinforce a person's feelings of helplessness. All are possible, and all can occur under the guise of helping. Therefore, it is important to remember that "deprofessionalized" help does not necessarily mean better help—different, perhaps; not necessarily better. Just as professionals do not necessarily deliver *quality* help, neither do the "new" helpers. While we noted in the first chapter how there were not enough professional helpers available to meet needs, the provision of other kinds of help simply means that more interactions are occurring. This says little about the *quality* of the interactions. How many are *truly helpful*?

A high-quality helping relationship consists of skilled and planned use of effective verbal and nonverbal behavior, a perceptive and accurate understanding of the helpee's situation, familiarity with helping strategies and theoretical knowledge about help-giving, and sensitivity to the ethical dilemmas involved. Helping of this type is deliberate and thoughtful. It is the careful use of the helper as a person, the sharing of self in a highly facilitative and purposeful way. It is indeed the sharing of resources, but the interpersonal resources shared are trust, acceptance, caring, and concern. Helping like this is not innate, nor does it come easily to most. Training and extensive experience are called for. It is our conviction that the skills, capabilities, and sensitivities that are described in the chapters of this book are necessary ingredients for *quality* helping.

These ingredients are integrated into a unique, idiosyncratic helping philosophy by the effective helper. This helping philosophy is developed gradually, with increased experience, further training, improved skills and especially with thoughtfulness. One's evolving helping philosophy is not accidental; it is deliberately and sensitively formulated, another mark of quality helping.

IN CLOSING

We started this chapter by asking you to foretell your future as a helper. Our own best guess about the future of helping others is that helping will happen in many circumstances, many kinds of helpees will receive help or give themselves help, and the kinds of problems that are brought to helpers will change to reflect the times. People will turn to their own local resources, and paraprofessionals and nonprofessionals will provide much of the direct helping services. Many new kinds of problems will be identified and individuals will embark on many different journeys of self-development. Despite all this chaos and change, helping will remain the essential human activity that it is. High-quality helping will occur when sincere, well-intentioned helpers carefully yet spontaneously use their helping skills to resolve their helpees' concerns and encourage their helpees to develop more fully, no matter what the setting.

References

Benjamin, A. *The helping interview.* Boston: Houghton Mifflin, 1969.
Benson, H. *The relaxation response.* New York: Avon, 1975.
Berne, E. *Games people play.* New York: Grove Press, 1964.
Bernstein, D. A., & Borkovec, T. D. *Progressive relaxation training.* Champaign, Ill.: Research Press, 1973.
Danish, S. J., D'Augelli, A. R., & Hauer, A. L. *Helping skills: A basic training program.* New York: Human Sciences Press, 1980.
Dworkin, E. P., & Dworkin, A. L. The activist counselor. *Personnel and Guidance Journal,* 1971, *49,* 748-753.
Egan, G. *The skilled helper.* Monterey, Calif.: Brooks/Cole, 1975.
Egan, G. *Interpersonal living: A skills/contract approach to human-relations training in groups.* Monterey, Calif.: Brooks/Cole, 1976.
Ekman, P., & Friesen, W. V. Nonverbal leakage and clues to deception. *Psychiatry,* 1969, *32,* 88-106.
Ellis, A., & Harper, R. A. *A new guide to rational living.* Englewood Cliffs, N.J.: Prentice-Hall, 1975.
Freudenberger, H. J. New psychotherapy approaches with teenagers in a new world. *Psychotherapy: Theory, Research, and Practice,* 1971, *8,* 38-43.
Gartner, A., & Riessman, F. *Self-help in the human services.* San Francisco: Jossey-Bass, 1977.
Halleck, S. *The politics of therapy.* New York: Science House, 1971.
Kell, B. L., & Mueller, W. L. *Impact and change.* New York: Appleton-Century-Crofts, 1966.
Knapp, M. L. *Nonverbal communication in human interaction.* New York: Holt, Rinehart & Winston, 1972.
Kohlberg, L. The development of children's orientation toward a moral order. *Vita Humana,* 1963, *6,* 11-33.
Kohlberg, L. Stage and sequence: The cognitive-developmental approach to socialization. In D. Goslin (Ed.), *Handbook of socialization theory and research.* Chicago: Rand McNally, 1969.
Kohlberg, L. Moral stages and moralization: The cognitive-developmental approach. In T. Lickona (Ed.), *Moral development and behavior: Theory, research, and social issues.* New York: Holt, Rinehart & Winston, 1976.

Mahl, G. F. Measuring the patient's anxiety during interviews from "expressive" aspects of his speech. *Transactions of the New York Academy of Sciences*, 1959, *21*, 249-257.

Maslow, A. H. *Toward a psychology of being*. New York: Van Nostrand Reinhold, 1968.

Mehrabian, A. *Silent messages*. Chicago: Aldine, 1968.

Rogers, C. R. The necessary and sufficient conditions of therapeutic personality change. *Journal of Consulting Psychology*, 1957, *21*, 95-103.

Rogers, C. R. Empathic: An unappreciated way of being. *The Counseling Psychologist*, 1975, *5*, 2-10.

Smith, R. E., & Zietz, D. *American social welfare institutions*. New York: John Wiley, 1970.

Sommer, R. *Personal space: The behavioral basis of design*. Englewood Cliffs, N.J.: Prentice-Hall, 1969.

Weinberger, P. E. (Ed.). *Perspectives on social welfare*. London: Macmillan, 1969.

Suggested Readings on Helping

The readings listed below are useful additional resources for learning more about different perspectives on helping others. No single view of helping (even ours!) is sufficient for a complete understanding of the kinds of problems people experience and the various methods of helping. It is recommended, therefore, that you sample some of the books below. Many are general introductions to helping or to different kinds of helping (marital counseling, family therapy, group work, and so forth). In choosing entries for this list, we sought books that were appropriate for individuals at a beginning level of experience in helping. We avoided highly technical books or summaries of research studies. (Both of these kinds of resources are essential as one becomes more knowledgeable and experienced!) We hope these listings help you consolidate and expand upon what you learned from reading *Helping Others*.

Ard, B. N., & Ard, C. C. (Eds.). *Handbook of marriage counseling.* Palo Alto, Calif.: Science and Behavior Books, 1969.
Arnold, L. E. (Ed.). *Helping parents help their children.* New York: Brunner/Mazel, 1978.
Avila, D. L., Combs, A. W., & Purkey, W. W. *The helping relationship sourcebook.* Boston: Allyn & Bacon, 1977.
Axline, V. *Play therapy.* New York: Ballantine Books, 1969.
Benjamin, A. *The helping interview.* Boston: Houghton Mifflin, 1969.
Benson, H. *The relaxation response.* New York: Avon, 1975.
Bernstein, D. A., & Borkovec, T. D. *Progressive relaxation training.* Champaign, Ill.: Research Press, 1973.
Brammer, L. M. *The helping relationship.* Englewood Cliffs: N.J.: Prentice-Hall, 1979.
Brown, J. H., & Brown, C. S. *Systematic counseling.* Champaign, Ill.: Research Press, 1977.

SUGGESTED READINGS

Carkhuff, R. R. *Helping and human relations* (2 vols.). New York: Holt, Rinehart & Winston, 1969.
Combs, A. W., Avila, D. L., & Purkey, W. W. *Helping relationships.* Boston: Allyn & Bacon, 1978.
Corey, G. *Theory and practice of counseling and psychotherapy.* Monterey, Calif.: Brooks/Cole, 1977.
Corey, G., & Corey, M. S. *Groups: Process and practice.* Monterey, Calif.: Brooks/Cole, 1977.
Corey, G., Corey, M. S., & Callanan, P. *Professional and ethical issues in counseling and psychotherapy.* Monterey, Calif.: Brooks/Cole, 1979.
Cormier, W. H., & Cormier, L. S. *Interviewing strategies for helpers: A guide to assessment, treatment, and evaluation.* Monterey, Calif.: Brooks/Cole, 1979.
Corsini, R. J. *Current psychotherapies.* Itasca, Ill.: Peacock, 1979.
Cowen, E. L., Gardner, E. A., & Zax, M. (Eds.). *Emergent approaches to mental health problems.* New York: Appleton-Century-Crofts, 1967.
Craighead, W. E., Kazdin, A. E., & Mahoney, M. J. *Behavior modification: Principles, issues, and applications.* Boston: Houghton Mifflin, 1976.
Dinkmeyer, D. *Group counseling.* Itasca, Ill.: Peacock, 1979.
Dugger, J. G. *The new professional: Introduction for the human services/mental health worker.* Monterey, Calif.: Brooks/Cole, 1975.
Egan, G. *The skilled helper.* Monterey, Calif.: Brooks/Cole, 1975.
Ellis, A., & Harper, R. A. *A new guide to rational living.* Englewood Cliffs, N. J.: Prentice-Hall, 1975.
Erickson, G. D., & Hogan, T. P. (Eds.). *Family therapy: An introduction to theory and technique.* Monterey, Calif.: Brooks/Cole, 1972.
Evans, D. R., Hearn, M. T., Uhlemann, M. R., & Ivey, A. E. *Essential interviewing: A programmed approach to effective communication.* Monterey, Calif.: Brooks/Cole, 1979.
Ferber, A., Mendelsohn, M., & Napier, A. *The book of family therapy.* New York: Science House, 1972.
Fischer, J. (Ed.). *Interpersonal helping: Emerging approaches for social work practice.* Springfield, Ill.: Charles C Thomas, 1973.
Foley, V. D. *An introduction to family therapy.* New York: Grune & Stratton, 1974.
Fullmer, D. W., & Bernard, H. W. *The school counselor-consultant.* Boston: Houghton Mifflin, 1972.
Gazda, G. M., Asbury, F. R., Balzer, F. J., Childers, W. C., & Walters, R. P. *Human relations development.* Boston: Allyn & Bacon, 1977.
Goodman, G. *Companionship therapy.* San Francisco: Jossey-Bass, 1972.
Gordon, T. *Parent effectiveness training.* New York: Peter H. Wyden, 1970.
Gottman, J. M., & Leiblum, S. R. *How to do psychotherapy and how to evaluate it.* New York: Holt, Rinehart & Winston, 1974.
Gottman, J. M., Notarius, C., Jonso, J., & Markman, H. *A couple's guide to communication.* Champaign, Ill.: Research Press, 1976.
Guerney, B. G., Jr. *Psychotherapeutic agents: New roles for nonprofessionals, parents, and teachers.* New York: Holt, Rinehart & Winston, 1969.
Guerney, B. G., Jr. *Relationship enhancement.* San Francisco: Jossey-Bass, 1977.
Gurman, A. S., & Rice, D. G. (Eds.). *Couples in conflict.* New York: Aronson, 1975.
Halleck, S. *The politics of therapy.* New York: Science House, 1971.
Harmon, L. W., Birk, J. M., Fitzgerald, L. E., & Tanney, M. F. *Counseling women.* Monterey, Calif.: Brooks/Cole, 1978.
Harper, R., Wiens, A., & Matarazzo, J. *Nonverbal communication.* New York: Wiley, 1978.

Henley, N. *Body politics.* Englewood Cliffs, N. J.: Prentice-Hall, 1977.
Hoffman, J. C. *Ethical confrontation in counseling.* Chicago: University of Chicago Press, 1979.
Holler, R. F., & DeLong, G. M. *Human services technology.* St. Louis, Mo.: C. V. Mosby, 1973.
Ivey, A. E., & Authier, J. *Microcounseling.* Springfield, Ill.: Charles C Thomas, 1979.
Ivey, A. E., & Simek-Downing, L. *Counseling and psychotherapy: Skills, theory, and practice.* Englewood Cliffs, N. J.: Prentice-Hall, 1980.
Johnson, D. W., & Johnson, F. P. *Joining together: Group therapy and group skills.* Englewood Cliffs, N. J.: Prentice-Hall, 1975.
Kanfer, F. H., & Goldstein, A. P. *Helping people change.* New York: Pergamon Press, 1975.
Kazdin, A. E. *Behavior modification in applied settings.* Homewood, Ill.: Dorsey Press, 1975.
Knapp, M. L. *Nonverbal communication in human interaction.* New York: Holt, Rinehart & Winston, 1972.
Krumboltz, J. D., & Thoresen, C. E. *Counseling methods.* New York: Holt, Rinehart & Winston, 1976.
Lange, A. J., & Jakubowski, P. *Responsible assertive behavior.* Champaign, Ill.: Research Press, 1976.
LeVine, E., & Padilla, A. M. *Crossing cultures in therapy.* Monterey, Calif.: Brooks/Cole, 1980.
Lewis, J. A., & Lewis, M. D. *Community counseling.* New York: Wiley, 1977.
Lieberman, M. A., Yalom, I. D., & Miles, M. B. *Encounter groups: First facts.* New York: Basic Books, 1973.
Mash, E. J., Hamerlynck, L. A., & Handy, L. C. *Behavior modification and families.* New York: Brunner/Mazel, 1976.
Mash, E. J., Handy, L. C., & Hamerlynck, L. A. *Behavior modification approaches to parenting.* New York: Brunner/Mazel, 1976.
Mehrabian, A. *Nonverbal communication.* Chicago: Aldine, 1972.
Miller, W. H. *Systematic parent training.* Champaign, Ill.: Research Press, 1975.
Okun, B. F. *Effective helping: Interviewing and counseling techniques.* North Scituate, Mass.: Duxbury, 1976.
Palmer, J. O. *A primer for eclectic psychotherapy.* Monterey, Calif.: Brooks/Cole, 1980.
Perez, J. F. *Family counseling.* New York: Van Nostrand Reinhold, 1979.
Pope, B. *The mental health interview.* Elmsford, N. Y.: Pergamon Press, 1979.
Rappaport, J. *Community psychology.* New York: Holt, Rinehart & Winston, 1977.
Rogers, C. R. *Client-centered therapy.* Boston: Houghton Mifflin, 1951.
Rogers, C. R. The characteristics of a helping relationship. *Personnel and Guidance Journal,* 1958, *37,* 6-16.
Rogers, C. R. *On becoming a person: A therapist's view of psychotherapy.* Boston: Houghton Mifflin, 1961.
Schlossberg, N. K., & Entine, A. D. *Counseling adults.* Monterey, Calif.: Brooks/Cole, 1977.
Schofield, W. *Psychotherapy: The purchase of friendship.* Englewood Cliffs, N. J.: Prentice-Hall, 1964.
Schulmann, E. D. *Intervention in human services.* St. Louis, Mo.: C. V. Mosby, 1978.
Shertzer, B., & Stone, S. C. *Fundamentals of counseling.* Boston: Houghton Mifflin, 1968.
Sundel, M., & Sundel, S. S. *Behavior modification in the human services.* New York: Wiley, 1975.

Thomas, E. J. (Ed.). *Behavior modification procedure: A sourcebook.* Chicago: Aldine, 1974.

Watson, D. L., & Tharp, R. G. *Self-directed behavior: Self-modification for personal adjustment.* Monterey, Calif.: Brooks/Cole, 1977.

Weitz, S. (Ed.). *Nonverbal communication.* New York: Oxford University Press, 1979.

Whiteley, J. M., & Flower, J. V. (Eds.). *Approaches to assertion training.* Monterey, Calif.: Brooks/Cole, 1978.

Whitlock, G. E. *Understanding and coping with real-life crises.* Monterey, Calif.: Brooks/Cole, 1978.

Wicks, R. J. *Counseling strategies and intervention techniques for the human services.* Philadelphia: Lippincott, 1977.

Wicks, R. J. *Human services: New careers and roles in the helping professions.* Springfield, Ill.: Charles C Thomas, 1978.

Williams, R. L., & Long, J. D. *Toward a self-managed life style.* Boston: Houghton Mifflin, 1975.

Index

Acceptance of helpee's feelings, 57
Addams, J., 2
Adjustment model of helping, 150, 151-153
Advice-giving, 79-83
  appropriate use of, 80
  and dependency, 81
  effective, 80-81
  main purpose of, 80
  and Program Planning Stage, 80
  and Reviewing Stage, 80
Affective responses, 62, 66-72
  and Clarification Stage, 71
  vs. content responses, 68-69
  effective, 69-71
  and empathy, 67-68
  and Entry Stage, 71
  and Exploration Stage, 71
Affective vocabulary, 70

Berne, E., 21
Body language, *see* Interactive cues; Kinesic cues, Nonverbal cues

Change, 4, 125
  and advice-giving, 79
  commitment to, 7-8
  and deep understanding, 121
  and helping strategies, 125

Change *(continued)*
  and influencing responses, 76-77
  and leading responses, 82
  and morality in helping, 149
  and open questions, 75-76
  remedial or enhancement, 7
  responsibility for, 7, 12
  and trust, 9
  and understanding, 103-105
Charity Organization Society, 3, 164
Clarification of problem, 127
Clothing, 41-42
  control over, 42
  as indicator of social group, 42
  as indicator of status, 41
Coit, S., 2
Communication:
  by continuing responses, 62
  evaluative vs. understanding, 55
  nonverbal cues, 29-32
  of sincerity, 28
  of willingness to listen, 29
Confrontation, 120-121
Content responses, 62, 63-66
  clarification function, 64
  and Clarification Stage, 71
  and defensiveness, 64
  effective, 64-66
  and Entry Stage, 71
  and Exploration Stage, 71
  as summary statement, 63

Continuing responses, 62-72
  affective responses, 62, 66-72
  content responses, 62, 63-66
  and the helping process, 71
"Core conditions" for helping, 56, 57-62

Danish, S. J., v
D'Augelli, A. R., v
Deep understanding, 106, 112-123
  bringing the message to awareness, 106, 114-116
  constructive collaboration, 106, 121-123
  exploration of meaning, 106, 116-119
  and goal attainment, 121
  identifying the message, 106, 112-114
  use of "door opening" response, 116-118
  working hypothesis, 119-120
Deprofessionalization of helping, 166-167
Differential reinforcing, 33-35
Distance, 50-51
Dworkin, A. L., 152
Dworkin, E. P., 152

Ekman, P., 32, 35
Empathy, 56-58
  and acceptance, 57
  and affective responses, 67-68
  vs. sympathy, 57-58
Enhancement model of helping, 6, 13, 150, 151-153
  assertiveness training, 6
  communication skills training, 6, 7
  parent training, 6
Environmental cues, 38, 50-52
  distance, 38, 50-51
  time, 38, 51-52
Ethics, 147-162
  and moral reasoning, 156-159
  vs. needs, 148
Eye contact, 42-45
  and clues about the relationship, 43

Eye contact *(continued)*
  and conversation flow, 43
  effective, 44-45
  and feedback, 43

Feedback, 6
Feelings of helpee, 56, 66-68
Freud, S., 3
Freudian revolution, 3
Friendly visitors, 2
Friesen, W. V., 32, 35

Gartner, A., 166
Genuineness, 56, 58-59
  and helper's use of self, 86
  "real" helper, 93
  "selfish" helper, 94-95
  and use of self-referent responses, 95
Global understanding, 105-106, 107-111
  affective description, 109-110
  impression-forming, 108-109
  rapid observation, 107-108
Gurteen, F. H., 3

Halleck, S., 151, 152, 154
Hauer, A. L., v
Helpee:
  defensiveness, 10
  definition, vi
  goals, 11-12
  strengths and weaknesses, 11-12
Helper:
  as model, 19, 20
  motivations, 15
  needs, 15
  nonprofessional and paraprofessional, 4, 13, 165-166
  personality of, 9
  professional, 3, 13
  and status quo, 161-162
Helping:
  action for change, 11
  basic elements, 8
  decisions regarding change, 11
  definition, 1, 5, 13, 144-145

Helping *(continued)*
  ethical concerns, 9
  as exploration, 11
  morality of, 159-162
  mystique of, 18-19
  need for, 163-165
  religious, 2-3
  "talking cure," 3
  and trust, 9
  values in, 155-156
Helping, model of, vi
  adjustment vs. enhancement, 150, 151-153
  advice-giving, 56
  facilitating self-growth, 58-59
  focus on feelings, 56
  and self-referent responses, 93-95
Helping goals, 5, 12, 149
  action, 12
  creating atmosphere, 11
  and deep understanding, 121, 122, 123
  helpee self-awareness, 57
  and leading responses, 82
  and moral decisions, 162
  and morality of helper, 148-156
  and pacing, 52
  and positive regard, 60
  self-disclosure, 62
  self-exploration, 62
  self-growth, 58
Helping philosophy, 1, 153-156, 168
  and moral reasoning, 156-159
  and sharing of values, 27
Helping process:
  Action-Taking Stage, 12, 82, 99, 101, 127
  assessment of problem, 127
  change in Program-Planning and Action-Taking Stages, 127
  Clarification Stage, 11, 34, 52, 71, 76, 101, 127
  demystification of, v
  Entry Stage, 11, 34, 52, 71, 89
  evaluation and reviewing process, 127
  Exploration Stage, 11, 34, 52, 71, 76, 127
  helping equation, 9, 13

Helping process *(continued)*
  Integration Stage, 11, 34, 76, 82, 99, 122, 127
  and problem-solving model, 127
  Program Planning Stage, 12, 34, 52, 76, 80, 82, 99, 101, 127
  Reviewing Stage, 52, 76, 80, 82, 101, 127
  skills-oriented approach, v, 13
  Termination Stage, 12, 52, 82, 101
  and use of questions, 76
  and use of self-disclosure responses, 99
Helping relationship:
  and beliefs, 26
  contractual aspect, 160-161
  control of, 20
  empathy in, 57
  and Entry Stage, 11
  exchange in, 17
  vs. friendship, 5-6
  games in, 21
  and helpee dependency, 19-20
  and helping strategies, 125
  purposes of, 6
  and values, 26
Helping strategies, 125-145
  general, 134-143
  giving feedback, 12
  rehearsal, 12, 138-139
  reinforcement of positive steps, 12
  reinforcement planning, 142-143
  relaxation, 139-140
  restructuring of thoughts, 140-142

Indigenous helping, 166
Industrial Revolution, 3
Influencing, 76-79
  and the helping process, 76
  and reinforcement, 77-78
Interactive cues, 38, 42-50
  body movement, 38, 42-45
  eyes, use of, 38, 42-45
  touch, 38, 45-46
  vocal quality, 38, 49-50

Kell, B. L., 15
Kinesic cues, 46-49

Kinesic cues *(continued)*
  affiliation, via smiling, 47–48
  disinterest, 49
  distancing, 49
  effective use of, 49
  liking, 46–47
  tension, 47
Knapp, M. L., 41
Kohlberg, L., 156–157

Leading responses, 62, 72–83

Maslow, A. H., 22–23
Mehrabian, A., 29
Morality of helping, 159–162
  and change, 149
  and helping goals, 148–156
  and social systems, 150–151
Moral reasoning in helping, 156–159
Motivations of helper, 15, 17
Mueller, W. L., 15

Needs of helper, 15, 16–21, 22–23
  for belonging, 25
  for closeness, 24
  and commitment to helping, 17
  for control, 16, 18–19, 21
  development of, 24–25
  effect of, on helping relationship, 18, 25
  for emotional closeness, 18
  vs. ethics, 148
  vs. helper behavior, 21–22
  for love and acceptance, 19
  and morality in helping, 159–160
  and nonconformity, 20
  for power, 18–19
  for prestige, 18
  for recognition, 24
Nonprofessional helpers, 4, 13, 165–166
Nonverbal attending behavior:
  conveying "withness," 32–33
  differential reinforcing, 33–35
  effective, 37–53
  encouraging exploration, 33

Nonverbal attending behavior *(continued)*
  and stages of the helping process, 34
Nonverbal cues:
  environmental, 38, 50–52
  head nod, 33
  interactive, 38, 42–50
  leakage, 35, 42–43, 48
  and moral help-giving, 154
  situational, 38, 39–42

Paraprofessionals, 4–5, 13, 165–166
Physical appearance, 39–40
Problem behavior, 128–131
  antecedents and consequences of, 132–134
  reinforcement of, 133–134
  and social conditions, 164
Problem-solving:
  assessment, 126–127, 128–134
  evaluation, 126–127, 143–144
  general behavior change methods, 137–143
  model of, 126, 127–128
  planning, 126–127, 134–137
  process of, 125, 126, 127–128
Psychoanalysis, 3

Questions, 72–76
  closed, 72–73
  forms to avoid, 76
  open, 72, 74–76
  and stages of helping process, 76

Rehearsal, 138–139
Reinforcement planning, 142–143
Relaxation, 139–140
Restructuring of thoughts, 140–142
Riessman, F., 166
Rogers, C. R., 56

Self-disclosure, 86–87, 95–99
  biographical, 95–96
  duration of, 95, 97–98
  guidelines for, 98–99

Self-disclosure *(continued)*
  intensity of, 95, 96-97
  personal, 96
  reciprocity effect, 91
  and stages of helping process, 99
Self-help, 166-167
Self-involving responses, 86-87, 100-102
  and confrontation, 100-101
  duration of, 100
  guidelines for, 101-102
  intensity of, 100
  and moral help-giving, 154
  and stages of helping process, 101
Self-referent responses, 67, 83, 85-102
  and Entry Stage, 89
  general effects of, 88
  modeling effect, 88, 91-93
  personal involvement effect, 88-90
  self-disclosure responses, 86-87, 95-99
  self-involving responses, 86-87, 100-102
  and stages of helping process, 99, 101
Settlement House, 2, 164
Sexism in helping, 153-154
Situational cues, 38-42
  clothing, 38, 41-42
  physical appearance, 38, 39-41
Smith, R. E., 2
Social systems, 150-151, 151-153
Starr, E. G., 2

Time, 51-52
  and control of interaction, 52
  pacing, 52
  and stages of the helping process, 52
  and status cues, 51
Touch, 45-46

Unconditional positive regard, 56, 59-60
Understanding:
  differences between global and deep, 107
  effective, 107
  as hypothesis-generating, 103-104
  process of, 105-107

Values:
  conflict in helping, 27
  and the helping relationship, 26
  and helping strategy, 27
Vocal quality:
  effective use of, 50
  and speech disturbances, 49-50
  tone of voice, 49
  and understanding, 49

Weinberger, P. E., 2

Zietz, D., 2